# 7 LEADERSHIP Imperatives from a

D1215584

# 7 LEADERSHIP Imperatives from a

## Joseph Robinson Jr.

**FOREWORD BY CLEOPHUS J. LaRUE**

**JUDSON PRESS**
PUBLISHERS SINCE 1824
VALLEY FORGE, PA

7 Leadership Imperatives from a Wild Man
© 2008 by Judson Press, Valley Forge, PA 19482-0851
All rights reserved.

No part of this publication may be reproduced, stored in a retrieval system, or transmitted in any form or by any means, electronic, mechanical, photocopying, recording, or otherwise, without the prior permission of the copyright owner, except for brief quotations included in a review of the book.

Judson Press has made every effort to trace the ownership of all quotes. In the event of a question arising from the use of a quote, we regret any error made and will be pleased to make the necessary correction in future printings and editions of this book.

Unless otherwise indicated, Scripture quotations in this volume are from the King James Version of the Bible.

Scripture quotations marked NKJV are taken from the New King James Version. Copyright © 1982 by Thomas Nelson, Inc. Used by permission. All rights reserved.

Portions of this book have been previously published as Joseph Robinson Jr., *Seven Leadership Imperatives from a Wild Man: John the Baptist Speaks* (Washington, DC: A. P. Foundation Press, 2005).

**Library of Congress Cataloging-in-Publication Data**

Robinson, Joseph, 1957–
   7 leadership imperatives from a wild man / Joseph Robinson, Jr. — 1st ed.
      p. cm.
   ISBN-13: 978-0-8170-1528-2 (pbk. : alk. paper) 1. Leadership—Religious aspects—Christianity. 2. John, the Baptist, Saint. I. Title. II. Title: Seven leadership imperatives from a wild man.
   BV4597.53.L43R63 2007
   253—dc22

                                                                 2007035241

Printed on recycled paper in the U.S.A.
First Printing, 2008.

*To my wife,*
*whom I affectionately refer to as "my teenager,"*
*for your unwavering love and support.*
*You lend purpose to all I do*
*and give meaning to my life.*
*Thank you.*

# CONTENTS

# FOREWORD

Leadership based on Scripture is so seriously lacking in so many churches that this book qualifies as an answer to prayer. In this compelling and forthright book, Joseph Robinson has taken on the challenge of providing simple principles designed to make the work of the church flow more smoothly. He lists for us seven "imperatives" that are simple to understand and easy to do. In fact, Robinson writes with such clarity that one wonders why such principles have not been put forth before. This is a must-read for all who desire to stand under the authority of the Word and lead in a biblically sound and theologically relevant manner. Anyone of any denominational background will find great value in following Robinson's outline of responsible leadership practices.

*7 Leadership Imperatives from a Wild Man* is filled with anecdotes and other slices of life that help the reader to identify with the points Robinson is making about particular aspects of leadership. This resource is part instruction, part practical guide, and part sermon, and Robinson has his eye on the leadership target throughout. It is readable, accessible, and teachable and can be used in small groups and Bible studies. It is filled with biblical illustrations and practical admonitions from the life of one who can best be characterized as a seasoned "churchman" in the finest sense of the term. I highly recommend this book for all who are interested in developing leadership in their church and in their personal journeys.

Cleophus J. LaRue
Professor of Preaching and Worship
Princeton Theological Seminary

# ACKNOWLEDGMENTS

This book is the product of my years as an administrator and the many leadership opportunities afforded me by people who saw the dormant potential. I am grateful to everyone who has encouraged me throughout this undertaking. While I cannot list each of you, I am compelled to acknowledge at least a few with sincerest gratitude:

*The Lord God,* for giving me inspiration, wisdom, and stamina.

*Rebecca Irwin-Diehl,* my editor at Judson Press, for your guidance and constant encouragement, as well as your skillful eye, resulting in a product that is far superior to that which I submitted.

*Rev. Alvin Q. Taylor,* my friend and brother who introduced me to the Judson Press family by way of Gale Tull. Without the instrumental intervention and advocacy of you both, this project may never have materialized.

*Richard H. Harris Jr.,* my deceased boss and mentor, who groomed, nurtured, and guided me. I will always cherish our bond of friendship and the lessons you imparted.

*Rev. Charles R. Meile Jr.,* my pastor, for the leadership opportunity you provided me as the former director of ministries. The experience was exhilarating and gave birth to this leadership model.

*My family,* for your love, encouragement, and unflagging confidence.

*Dennis Knepper,* my brother in the Lord, for your technical assistance with preparing the final manuscript for submission.

*Clifton Edwards,* for your critical feedback that helped bring focus to my thesis.

# INTRODUCTION

eadership is a term that evokes far-ranging images depending on one's background and orientation. Our minds gravitate to recollections of great leaders of the past as diverse as Abraham Lincoln, George Washington, Alexander the Great, Hannibal, Hatshepsut (female pharaoh of Egypt), Joan of Arc, Eleanor Roosevelt, Shaka Zulu, and Martin Luther King Jr. For many, such leaders are the standard by which all others are judged. However, noteworthy leadership is not just found among the royal, renowned, and revered. All over the world people from various walks of life are leading in ways that are worthy of emulation.

This book examines the characteristics of a person who lived a life that was exemplary yet enigmatic, productive yet puzzling, charismatic yet a curiosity. He was an only child, born to God-fearing parents. He had only a basic education. He never left his hometown. He had a unique diet and wore unfashionable clothing. He was loathed by some and loved by others. He died before age thirty-five by decapitation. Still he managed to leave an indelible imprint on history. The question begging to be asked is what can we learn about leadership from a man who ends up losing his head?

John the Baptist was the son of aged parents who had longed to have children but to no avail. According to the Gospel of

Luke, God honored the parents and assured them they would have a child even though their biological functions had long since abated. The angel Gabriel appeared to the father-to-be, Zacharias, and informed him that his wife, Elisabeth, would indeed bear a son who would serve as forerunner and precursor to the much anticipated Messiah. Fast-forward thirty years and we find the child, John, grown up and his parents most likely deceased. Like his priestly father, he too is in the service of the Lord, but his temple is without walls. His robes are not made of fine fabric but of weathered camel's hair. His daily sustenance is not derived from wave offerings, but from wild locusts and honey. He has but one sermon: "Repent!"

> ... The fire of God
> Fills him. I never saw his like; there lives
> No greater leader.
> —*Alfred Lord Tennyson*, Idylls of the King: Lancelot and Elaine

Invariably when I speak for a wide array of audiences, I am asked how it is that I derived leadership insight from the life of John the Baptist. This is a fair question given the brevity of historical information on this man of intrigue. Aside from the gospel accounts in the Bible and a brief mention by the early Jewish historian Josephus Flavius, we have little information on the life of John the Baptist. My answer is simply this: I believe that whatever we do, we bring our experiences, training, and education to the table and view everything through those lenses, including a reading of the Scriptures. As a midlevel manager for twenty-six years, I acquired extensive experience in the areas of strategic planning, employee development, and leadership. Several years ago, while reading the account of John the Baptist, I saw a pattern emerging that was spellbinding. I began to see a simple man whose life exhibited some fundamental and easily applied principles. I felt so compelled that

I termed these leadership attributes "imperatives"—commands, incontestable requirements. When embraced, these imperatives will transform a person into an effective leader. Application of these imperatives may not elevate a person to the stature of a Winston Churchill or Abraham Joshua Heschel, but they will provide a framework for daily living that is impactful and fulfilling.

The majority of published books about John the Baptist are scholarly and attempt to harmonize the gospel accounts and wrestle with John's relation to Jesus and his theological significance as the Elijah of his day. I do not even pretend to be equipped to contribute to this existing body of scholarly discourse. My premise is that John's life—the little we know of it—serves as a model of effective leadership for leaders at all levels. Consequently, I am constrained to use a profusion of examples, both biblical and secular, to illustrate the universality of John's imperatives.

This book is not a theological defense of any particular denominational form of governance. Instead, it provides a common language and framework for discussing leadership that builds upon the reader's intuitive understanding. As you intently read the successive pages, you will see how this singularly focused man turned the entire region right side up. I hope that as you read and reflect on these seven imperatives, you will discover the possibilities for effective leadership within yourself as exhibited by this wild man of priestly descent.

# Sure

There was a man sent from God, whose name was John. The same came for a witness, to bear witness of the Light, that all men through him might believe. He was not that Light, but was sent to bear witness of that Light.

—JOHN 1:6-8

We all struggle with the question of purpose. Some may take exception, but at least 26 million or more purchasers of Rick Warren's *The Purpose Driven Life* seem to agree. Even the most successful among us have joked, "I still don't know what I want to be when I grow up." Others are fortunate to find their place in life and function without this nagging uncertainty.

John the Baptist was clear on three key issues: his *parentage*, his *purpose*, and his *purview*. A review of the text for this imperative, "Be sure," indicates that he originated, or was sent, from God (John 1:6). John's birth was predicted and proclaimed by an angel believed to be Gabriel. The angel had declared that John was to live a consecrated lifestyle and prepare the hearts of men and women to receive the Messiah (Luke 1:5-25). This knowledge shaped John's outlook toward life and provided a compass for his direction.

Today we understate the value of knowing our origin and history. Some of us have never bothered to determine why our parent(s) gave us the name we carry. Many of us never learn cousin "Bo-Bo's" real name until the funeral. We never bother to ask because we don't view it as important. Yet names, family traditions, and heirlooms provide valuable insight into that which makes us who we are. My life has been impacted by my southern North Carolina ancestry. I tend to view and analyze events through my perspective as both a native Carolinian and a Northerner raised and educated in Pennsylvania. I am an amalgam of Northern ambition and Southern hospitality, frenetic with good manners and respect for others.

---

**Self-reverence, self-knowledge, self-control,–**
**These three alone lead life to sovereign power.**

—*Alfred Lord Tennyson*, Œnone

---

The text reveals that John also understood his *purpose*, which was "to bear witness of the Light, that all men through him might believe" (John 1:7). He was crystal clear about the job assigned to him and never wavered, because he understood what was riding on his actions. He was compelled to bear witness because of the lives and souls of men and women at stake. Many of us find it difficult or at least awkward to consistently witness to others about our faith. I suspect that is because we don't dwell enough on the consequences for those whom we neglect to win. When you grasp the full import of the task assigned to you, it no longer becomes mundane. Cleaning toilets at the local airport takes on another level of responsibility when you truly realize that your disinfecting diligence could well prevent an outbreak of disease.

Finally, the text reveals that John knew his boundaries, or *purview*. "He was not that Light, but was sent to bear witness of that Light" (John 1:8). I once heard a preacher friend of mine say that every man would do well to recognize his own limitations. The profundity of this statement must not be overlooked. John had no illusions about his role and was comfortable with it. Generally, whenever there is dissension in the camp, it can be traced to a clash of role boundaries. Sometimes it boils down to rebellion against authority. Some just can't stomach taking direction from those in authority. What follows is a clashing of wills and ineffective ministry. No one knows everything, and we can all learn from someone else. The sooner we accept that we are not the ultimate fount of knowledge, the sooner we can learn to stay within our given scope of duties and leave those outside our scope to someone else.

Mother Teresa comes to mind as someone with clear purpose. As a preadolescent she felt the call to serve God, and at age eighteen she left home to become a nun. She attained her status as a nun in 1931 at the age of twenty-one, serving the poor and indigent of Calcutta, India, until her death at age eighty-seven on September 5, 1997. She was so committed to her work that with the approval of the Vatican, she began her own order in 1950, the Missionaries of Charity.

Another example of purpose and certainty is the fictional character John Henry, who was romanticized in the folk song bearing his name. You may recall that John Henry was a former black slave who waged a contest with a steam-driven drilling machine in a symbolic fight of human efforts to withstand the machine age and its elimination of the need for human labor. One thing that is of significance in our discussion of leadership is found in the first stanza of the folk song:

When John Henry was a little baby
Sitting on his pappy's knee
He picked up a hammer and a piece of steel
And said, "Hammer, you'll be the death of me."[1]

From birth John Henry was sure of his purpose and his mission in life. Once you are sure that you are doing what you were created to do, nothing else matters—not even failure, because it is part of the refining process to develop, improve, and grow you.

---

I'm doing what I think I was put on this earth to do. And I'm really grateful to have something that I'm passionate about and that I think is profoundly important.

—*Marian Wright Edelman*

---

Most of us, however, are not so assured that we are in the place uniquely prepared for us. How can we know for sure? Well, trial and error is still a proven method, but it can be expensive in terms of time, resources, and the patience of others who wait for you to "find yourself." Another alternative is the use of diagnostic tools to help you assess your makeup, personality, spiritual gifts, and vocational inclination. These tools are designed to provide a profile that gives a clear indication of your natural gifts, abilities, interests, and personality style. They essentially provide answers to the following questions:

What is the one thing I enjoy doing more than anything else?

What is the thing I am usually doing when I lose track of time?

What is the one thing I'd enjoy doing if I didn't have to work for a living?

What is the one thing I'd do for free if I could do it all of the time?

These tools are comprehensive and effective if the respondent is honest with himself or herself when completing the assessment. Another way to ascertain your purpose is to ask God. If I want to know something about my car, I go back to the manufacturer. Likewise, if I want to know what God intends for me, I ask him. He alone knows what role I am to play in this cosmic theater of life. So consult God through much prayer and utilize available tools in your search for your life's calling.

When thinking about relying on our own tools or resources, I recall the discourse Jesus had with his disciples as recorded in Matthew 16:13-15: "Whom do men say that I the Son of man am? And they said, Some say that thou art John the Baptist: some, Elias; and others, Jeremias, or one of the prophets. He saith unto them, But whom say ye that I am?"

While the interpretation and intent of this passage is universally understood, we can draw from it without much difficulty to make an application to the subject of determining one's purpose. Borrowing from Jesus' line of questioning, I would ask, "What do people say you are good at?" Many times others will recognize your unique abilities long before you do simply because to you the gift or skill is so natural that you assume everyone can do what you do. You are not being indifferent or taking the gift for granted; rather, you have a genuine unawareness of your effectiveness. So when others compliment you on how well you interact with children or how well you sing, paint, dance, speak, or act, you may initially find their compliments surprising. My own experience confirms this. I had been told many times by others that my letter-writing skills were above average. However, because composing letters was fun and stimulating for me, I didn't feel that my output was unique. Of course I felt I made a quality effort but not necessarily a unique or noteworthy one. It wasn't until my writing became publishable that I began to believe what others had been saying all along.

The other question we can glean from Jesus' line of questioning to his disciples is, "What do you say you are good at?" Having others recognize your abilities isn't enough; you must also self-evaluate and determine your competencies. Answering this question requires honesty, not hubris. Hubris is excessive pride, arrogance, or self-confidence, the kryptonite over which honesty cannot prevail.

> When you are feeling most confident, what activity are you generally engaged in and what role are you performing?
>
> When engaged in an activity, do the results confirm your feelings about your effectiveness?
>
> What are the things that come naturally to you?
>
> What are the activities you enjoy, no matter how tedious or time consuming?

It is no accident that these two fundamental questions derived from Jesus' inquiry work in concert. Asserting "I'm a good singer" is of little value when no one is willing to corroborate your viewpoint. Some people sing because they are extraordinarily gifted; others sing only because they are happy. Face it, we are all vocal virtuosos in our private shower stalls or when singing along with our favorite recording artist. But once the music stops or the shower jet is hushed, reality shows up to remind us that we were wise not to pursue singing as our means of making a living. So, determining your purpose requires personal reflection coupled with validation from those around you.

I know of a man who was expected on his job to interact with clients and assist them in troubleshooting their business processes. He did not excel in this job because he was not extroverted by nature. Consequently, his inability to establish immediate rapport with his clients resulted in his motivation being questioned, creating frustration for both him and his supervisor. A crisis in the workload caused him to be reassigned temporarily to an independent office-support function, and to the surprise of all, he flourished. He was finally doing what he was suited for. How many of us are floundering in positions that we know are not right for us?

We will each sometimes find the pathway to purpose obstructed and often frustrating. What kind of education should a high-school graduate pursue—one that satisfies parental expectations, one that appeals to natural gifts, one that offers greater income and advancement, or one that promises the most personal satisfaction? When two people decide to marry, how will they make decisions about where to live, whose education to prioritize, and which job to follow—hers because it is more lucrative or his because it is more fulfilling? When two working professionals decide to expand their family, how do they juggle the new responsibility of providing for the emotional and economic needs of children while also sustaining a commitment to their vocational sense of purpose?

**It's hard to lead a cavalry charge if you think you look funny on a horse.**

*—Adlai Stevenson*

It's unfortunate that when life confronts us with change, we make our decisions hastily, out of desperation, fear, or misplaced priorities. The phenomenon commonly called "midlife crisis" is usually linked to a nagging feeling that we have wasted the better part of our productive years engaged in activities that did not bring fulfillment or success. If we would seize the opportunity to ponder our purpose at key times of transition, we might be better able to adjust to the new phase of life, confident that we had striven in our field of calling and passion.

When you face a critical transition or decision, keep in mind that life mirrors nature, and so just as we enjoy the four seasons of winter, spring, summer, and fall, so will we go through life seasons. What may have been our purpose in one life season may not be so in the next. And while it is true that God warned humanity in the beginning that our work would not be easy— "In the sweat of thy face shalt thou eat bread, till thou return unto the ground; for out of it wast thou taken: for dust thou art, and unto dust shalt thou return" (Genesis 3:19)—it is also a fact of nature that there are times in nature's life cycle when the fruit of our labor is more easily harvested! We will revisit this idea about life's seasons in imperative 5, "Be Complementary."

Instead of trusting God and these natural life cycles, panic-stricken, we attempt to assuage our feelings and rationalize the insufficiency of our chosen path by comparing our station in life with that of our peer group, taking inventory of our plusses and minuses. We engage in ego-gratifying (or stultifying) comparisons with the Joneses next door. The late Dr. E. V. Hill said, "Don't worry about keeping up with the Joneses—the Smiths are doing fine." I encourage you to reflect on those things that make you giddy with passion and, from this point on, to determine to go through life living rather than merely existing. When it's all over, none of us will die with an empty in-box; none of us will lament that we didn't spend more time in the office; none of us will consider the limited time we invested in our families adequate.

To illustrate, I heard the story told of a Northern businessman on vacation in the Caribbean islands who spent the better part of the week observing a native fisherman go out in the morning, only to return around noon and spend the balance of the day interacting with his children. After three days of observation, the businessman commented to the fisherman, "If you would fish a full day, you'd increase your catch." The fisherman responded, "Yes, but then what would I do?" Excited that he had the fisherman's attention, the businessman continued, "Well, if you caught a full day's load, you could purchase a larger boat." The fisherman responded, "Yes, but then what would I do?" Becoming more animated, the businessman responded, "Well if you got a larger boat, you could hire some helpers." The fisherman responded, "Yes, and then what would I do?" Almost with delirium the businessman continued, "Well if you hired workers, you could establish an export business to the United States." The fisherman responded, "Yes, but then what would I do?" The businessman replied with a superior air of satisfaction, "You could then become successful and wealthy and spend the day with your family." The fisherman simply nodded and said, "I see—but aren't I doing that now?" He already had a firm grasp on what was important and placed a high premium on quality time with his family. We would do well to learn from this fisherman.

## Use Your Auditory Filter

It amazes me how a mother can be consumed with multiple tasks yet hear her child's urgent plea for help over the din. A school teacher immediately gets to the source of a sudden disruption, correctly identifying the culprit who, to a classroom visitor, would have been indiscernible. A pastor wading through a throng of parishioners detects a need in the voice of one while perceiving an unspoken need in the body language of another. In each of these situations, the person uses a *filter* to tune out background noises and listen actively to what is essential. To hear God coaxing you toward your destiny, you also must ignore background noises.

The cure for cancer or AIDS may be lying dormant within some child or adult at this very moment, but for too long he or she has permitted others to squelch that inner urging to pursue his or her dreams and aspirations. Rather than trusting self and God, this person listens to background noise and sits on haunches of unbelief. How many times have we heard celebrities in the entertainment industry declare that the only thing they ever desired to do was to pursue their craft? Likewise, those same celebrities will readily tell you of the many individuals, especially those closest to them, who told them to "stop dreaming and get a real job." Not following their hearts would have resulted in lives of dreams deferred—what Langston Hughes compared to a dried-up raisin in the sun.[2]

The importance of following one's dreams was no more evident than in an experience I had with a former coworker. He was a bright, young, energetic industrial engineer who contributed tremendously to our organization. After about four years of service, however, he announced he had been accepted as an officer in one of the federal law enforcement agencies. Knowing his mild disposition, we were all surprised. But it was clear from his excitement that he was redirecting his life and moving toward his true center. I recall remarking to him, "Your parents must be thrilled, given that they paid for an engineering degree." He responded with a very insightful story. He had two older brothers who also became engineers, mechanical and electrical, respectively. Today one is a military police officer and the other is a cross-country truck driver! Essentially, he and his brothers initially chose "safe" paths while ignoring their passions. Fortunately, all three recognized what they were doing early on and took the courageous step to adjust their auditory filters and listen to their hearts.

---

**No one, Eleanor Roosevelt said, can make you feel inferior without your consent. Never give it.**

—*Marian Wright Edelman*

---

I have a personal friend who today is the consummate praise and worship leader, serving as the pastor of worship at his church. He has always had considerable talent as a singer and, like most, has entertained aspirations of fame, fortune, and celebrity in secular music. He never regarded himself much as a public speaker and would choose singing over public speaking anytime without fail. But later in life he was given an opportunity by his senior pastor to assume the position of pastor of worship, and almost immediately he flourished! He has become eloquent in speech, gifted in pointing the congregants toward Jesus in the spirit of worship, and inspirational and encouraging in his weekly pronouncements from the podium. He is operating within his gifting and fully living out the precepts of imperative 1, "Be sure."

In the 1967 movie *To Sir with Love*, Sidney Poitier plays a school teacher in a British school who is assigned a very unruly classroom of students. While laboring with the students, he is simultaneously applying for more prestigious positions elsewhere. As time elapses he begins to become emotionally committed to the students' development. One day he gets the long-awaited job offer and announces his intentions to resign from his post with the school. But something within gnaws at him until he realizes that he is most needed in his current post; it is at that school he will make the greatest impact on the lives of children already deemed incorrigible. And so he symbolically tears his job offer in two and resigns himself to "saving the children." It is a poignant movie that illustrates clearly imperative 1, "Be sure."

Another movie similar in theme was released in the 1990s starring Richard Dreyfus, titled *Mr. Holland's Opus*. In this movie an aspiring composer takes a temporary post as a high school music teacher while planning to write his defining collection of musical works—an opus. Instead, thirty years go by, the opus is still incomplete, and due to budget constraints the entire music staff is released. Holland reflectively confesses, "I got dragged into this thirty years ago kicking and screaming, and now it's the only thing I want to do." On his final day, the school throws a surprise farewell celebration attended by many of his former students, most notably a fledgling clarinetist he had nurtured who returns to his celebration as the state governor. She remarks, "Mr. Glenn Holland became neither rich nor famous for his symphony, but he achieved success far above riches; we are the notes in your symphony and the melody of your life." It is a compelling cinematic depiction of life as it is truly lived when we follow our inner voices and go hard after our passion. *Be sure!*

One day I had to take a dose of my own advice. For twenty-six years I worked for state government in an organization that strove for excellence. I was fortunate to attain a responsible position of leadership with a very talented and diverse team of managers. My intention was to work the required thirty-five years of service for full retirement benefits and live the remainder of my life traveling and seeing the world. Now I can see fully the living truth of the passage that says that if we will delight ourselves in the Lord, he will give us the desires of our hearts (Psalm 37:4). After a modicum of success in November 2005 with publishing my writing, I began to review our overall financial portfolio and contemplate an early retirement to pursue my passion to write and teach. After considerable prayer and much study of various financial scenarios, my wife and I made the decision to retire early—on January 27, 2006. Yes, we both retired on the same day!

I should tell you that many were surprised and a few were disturbed, but most were genuinely excited that we were taking such a bold step. I felt certain it was the right move to make and that God had confirmed the decision. Yet not a day went by that first year that I didn't secretly question whether I had acted impulsively. Fortunately, every time those doubts crept forward, I would adjust my auditory filter and turn to the promises in the Scriptures or a strong word of support from my unflappable wife. Just when I needed reassurance, God would move on some organization's heart to invite me to speak. The greatest of all assurances occurred when after just eleven months into our retirement Judson Press offered to publish the book you now read. Had I succumbed to the voices of unbelief and concern about finances, I would have missed the blessing reserved for me.

Having mentioned finances, I will share that we went from a six-figure yearly household income to slightly under $50,000. Of course, when we retired we were able to reduce most of our major debt, but the mortgage remained as well as the looming college expenses. So, as the head of the household and the one who got us into this, I felt immense pressure at times. However, as I said, at those times I adjusted my auditory filter and tuned into station WCGD—What Can't God Do?

## Am I Ready for This?

If we are honest, we all are struggling to stay one pace ahead of an unsettling failure when those around us are counting on us to deliver. John Eldredge opines in his book *Wild at Heart* that "every man is haunted by the question, am I really a man? Have I got what it takes . . . when it counts?"[2] Even epic heroes like Moses were at times gripped with this fear and uncertainty. How many times did he find himself facing impossible odds on the exodus journey, seeking God in prayer, saying, "Lord, what now?" If you don't think he was fearful when the Israelites found their pathway to freedom blocked by a raging Red Sea while the chariots of Egypt hurtled behind them in pursuit, then take off your Hollywood eyeglasses and get real. Moses was scared! And you would be too. Only days earlier he had triumphantly escorted the nearly two million freed people from Egypt, and now he was faced with the specter of having led them to certain death. Of course we know the story has a victorious ending, but it illustrates that at some level we are all fearful of failing.

It takes guts and some lost sleep to contemplate the kinds of mega-mergers we read about in the headlines, such as the Time Warner and AOL alliance. These well-meaning leaders are dreamers with great vision, who hope that they have the wherewithal to make the thing work. They do not want to fail. Nor do their shareholders want them to.

Many times, failing is inevitable for our growth and development. Who among us hopped on a bicycle for the first time and immediately graduated to riding with no hands before first experiencing a wobbly and toppling encounter (or two) with the pavement? Failing shortens our learning curve. I have found, however, that one way to minimize our failures is to be sure we are engaged in what we are called to do. Sometimes we fail simply because we are not doing what we were uniquely and wonderfully made to do. Once you have found your niche, it is very liberating. And even then, if you should fail—and you invariably will—it is just a refining process to hone your skills. I don't doubt that there were times John grew tired and the weight of the ostracism seemed unbearable. Undoubtedly, his first message was a bit rough, but in time he refined his message to the point that people flocked to heed his warnings. All of the missteps were endurable because he knew beyond any doubt that this was the work he was specifically called to perform.

Finding one's purpose is the path to real and lasting fulfillment. When Jesus declared, "I am come that they might have life, and that they might have it more abundantly" (John 10:10), his words encompassed many things, including a life of meaning and purpose. Great caution should be taken to ensure that you never see life as merely a vehicle by which you become rich and affluent. Rather, you should see life as an opportunity to make a difference. When you do this, all the other things follow. Jesus admonished his followers, "Seek ye first the kingdom of God, and his righteousness; and all these things shall be added unto you" (Matthew 6:33). Today we are bombarded with images of wealth and prosperity and duped into believing that they are ours for the taking in the spirit of boxing promoter Don King's assertion, "Only in America!" We are made to feel inadequate and incomplete by virtue of the material possessions we don't have and the luxurious vacations we don't take. This is a serious malady of the present era, and it runs counter to everything God's Word teaches us about quality living. The remedy is unselfish service to others, utilizing the gifts and abilities given to you by God.

---

**The secret of success is constancy to your purpose.**
—*Benjamin Disraeli*

---

If following God's plan for your life results in fame and financial gain, thank him for his favor and use the gain for the good of society. Following God's plan for your life may not result in fame and gain, but it will result in fulfillment and contentment. On a related note, we often feel that if we had more money, our lives would be simpler and easier. In actuality, the amount of money we accumulate is never the problem, but rather how we manage what has been given to us. So poor money handling forces the need to work harder to cover the shortfall, even at the expense of not pursuing the thing(s) that enliven us most. If you are like me, you are challenged each payday to get your ends to meet rather than crisscross. I have an uncle on my father's side of the family who has done reasonably well financially by living extraordinarily frugally while saving systematically. He counsels me often about the proper use of money. One of his favorite admonitions is to recall the Twenty-third Psalm, "I shall not *want*." He contends that anyone can retire early to pursue their true passion if they simply quit wanting! While it would be a challenge for most to live as sparingly as he does, his advice is on point.

Our obligation is to seek our purpose, and once we find it, to pursue it with passion and persistence. Bill Gates, formerly the richest man in the world, never had that distinction as his goal; rather, it was the fortuitous by-product of a life fixated on his passion. Am I denouncing wealth? No! I'm contending that the acquisition of self-serving wealth should never be the motivation for what we do. In Coretta Scott King's autobiography, *My Life with Martin Luther King, Jr.*, she quotes Horace Mann, the founder of her alma mater, Antioch College, who challenged the first graduating class to "be ashamed to die until you have won some victory for humanity!"[3] This is what Jesus intends when he responds to the question, "Who is my neighbor?" (see Luke 10:29-37). And it is also embedded in his declaration, "Greater love hath no man than this, that a man lay down his life for his friends" (John 15:13).

Each of us has an obligation to fearlessly and relentlessly determine our life's purpose. For example, as a church leader you have to be absolutely convinced that you are in the right ministry. I sang in our mass choir until I attended a music workshop and the lecturer began to stress how devoted one must be to the craft of singing, including securing private voice lessons if necessary. It gave me pause, and I came to the conclusion the following week that singing is not (any longer) something I feel compelled to do. While I may sing better than some, it is not the thing that most enthralls me. So I resigned. It was a huge decision for me, because I had sung in choirs most of my life and even directed several over the course of twenty years. To some this would be a surprising disclosure, but there is an explanation, alluded to previously, that will be addressed under imperative 5, "Be Complementary."

The message John the Baptist provides with imperative 1, "Be sure," is that once you fully recognize where you belong, pursue your goals with all the strength and zeal God has given you and never waver. Wavering can occur in either of two ways: (1) you can fail to believe God has uniquely assigned you to a certain work and consequently choose to run from your calling, or (2) you can respond to your calling but occasionally deviate and move into arenas that actually detract from your purpose. In the next chapter we will see how John avoided the latter pitfall by remaining resolute and focused.

## Points to Consider

**1.** How essential is it to determine our calling or purpose in life?

**2.** Does the fatalist who says, "What will be, will be," have a defensible perspective?

**3.** What do others say that you are good at?

**4.** What do you feel you are good at?

**5.** What would you do to make a contribution to society if you did not have to work for a living?

**6.** Whom do you personally know who exemplifies imperative 1, "Be sure"?

**7.** How would your life to this point have been different if you had applied this imperative?

# Focused

> Then said they unto him, Who art thou? that we
> may give an answer to them that sent us. What
> sayest thou of thyself? He said, I am the voice of
> one crying in the wilderness, Make straight the
> way of the Lord, as said the prophet Esaias.
> —JOHN 1:22-23

John the Baptist clearly demonstrates imperative 2, "Be focused." John was at the river preaching and baptizing people when the religious leaders, attempting to understand the reason for John's popularity, asked him to identify himself. He declared without any equivocation that he was just the voice sent to prepare for the one who was to come. Scripture says he declared, "I am not the Christ" (John 1:20).

Put yourself in John's shoes. If you were able to captivate the attention of hundreds of people in your city, to the point that even the mayor and every cleric in the city came to see you, wouldn't your head swell just a little bit? Be honest. Most of us would be very smug, I'm sure, but not John. How many of us could stay focused despite all the accolades others might heap upon us and say, "I am not the one"?

Because of John's popularity among the people, the ruling religious hierarchy sent a delegation to confront John and ask him to identify himself and his purpose. The rulers wanted to be sure John was not a reincarnated prophet or other mystic, so the delegation needed a viable response to take back to them. John proceeded to tell them that he was indeed of the same ilk as the prophet Elijah, with a similar message of preparation for the coming of the Lord. John could have wavered from his calling and denied his purpose. Or he could have concluded that the gawking, ridicule, challenging, and questioning were not worth it and chosen another vocation.

It is tempting to opt out of our destiny when it is fraught with challenges and uncertainty. Take Jonah, for instance. When commissioned by God to preach deliverance to the citizens of Nineveh, Jonah permitted his prejudices to interfere with his purpose. He opted to ignore his mission and hop a boat headed the other way, traveling where it suited him rather than God. John, however, implores us to follow God's calling for us. When you have discovered your purpose, you actually become free of uncertainty as to why you have been created. Discovering your purpose is liberating and affirming!

---

**The very essence of leadership is that you have to have a vision.**

*—Theodore Hesburgh*

---

Applauding someone too generously is dangerous, because if that person is not grounded and mature, he or she will begin to believe the press clippings. John was no rookie. He was a seasoned, hardened worker who had held up under ridicule, gawking, and criticism. Moreover, he never lost focus on his mission. Have you ever heard that all-too-familiar declaration made to an ardent church worker possessing charisma and good oratorical skills: "You're going to preach someday"? An immature Christian can easily begin to ponder these compliments secretly until he or she is finally convinced that "perhaps the people are correct" and then declare a ministerial calling on his or her life. That person falls victim to the old adage: "Some were sent, and some just went."

## I'll Do It!

Do you know people who seem to have their hands in everything at all times? No matter when you see them, they are hurrying and scurrying to the next task, meeting, conference, practice, rehearsal, appointment, or engagement. You wonder how they manage to juggle it all. You may discover that such persons are so stretched that they are virtually ineffective. Somewhere along the way they lost their focus. If you are so busy that you cannot give of yourself to complete an assigned endeavor effectively, you are too busy or are misplaced in ministry or function.

Some people are very adept at multitasking. They are extremely organized and systematic in the way they approach a task with laser focus. Once the planned milestone is reached or the project is completed, they move efficiently to the next task or project. It is not about this kind of individual that I am speaking. My thrust is the "willing worker" who for many reasons takes on more than can be handled.

For instance, most of us, especially church people, have a natural tendency to hesitate to say no when asked to take on yet another task. We somehow feel less than a team player if we don't chip in. We think, *After all, everyone else in the church is engaged in multiple ministries, so who am I to complain?* A single mother with four children works the food pantry, sings in the choir, teaches a class, and drives the church van. When you are surrounded with examples of others sacrificing so much of their personal time, you feel compelled to do likewise.

For some of us, being asked to take on more and more is an ego booster. Essentially, we are intoxicated with being asked to do more than we can manage. What a warped pathway to self-actualization and fulfillment! We feel that the busier we are, the more our time is in demand, the more crowded our planners, the more hectic our pace—then the more we are engaged and fighting in the struggle. For some this busyness borders on a martyr's mentality that says that it is my duty to work tirelessly for the cause even if (or until) it kills me. If my family suffers due to my unavailability, that is a cost of service, an occupational hazard if you will. All that matters is that I work "until the Lord calls me home."

As long as I volunteer to coach the Little League teams, logging countless hours of practice and competition, spurring young boys and girls to excellence while my own unathletic child sits at home aching for my approval even if only tacit, then it is worth the sacrifice (to me). If my children are "dragged" to church five of seven days because of my ministry commitments, even at the expense of a home life that should consist of consistent bonding time, homework assistance, recreation, and instruction, it is acceptable because, after all, "only what you do for Christ will last." I am suggesting that when we are focused as John the Baptist teaches by this imperative, our lives have balance. We sort out the extraneous from the essential.

---

**There's nothing more demoralizing than a leader who can't clearly articulate why we're doing what we're doing.**

*—James Kouzes and Barry Posner*

---

Before I leave this issue, I think it warrants some discussion as to what causes us to become heavily involved in something to the detriment of other equally, if not more important, things in our lives. Make no mistake about it, some people have a genuine sense of urgency as embodied in imperative 1, "Be sure."

Some activists, clergy, politicians, and other public servants are driven by a sense of purpose and immediacy. They feel as if a window of opportunity may soon close, and hence they haven't a moment to lose. While the same collateral damage due to neglect results, it is beyond their control; something within compels them to charge ahead single-mindedly, recognizing the benefits to be realized if they successfully attain their goal.

However, in more cases than we choose to admit, something more self-serving is afoot. The antagonist uses our pride as the vehicle to take us off course and cause imbalance in our lives. We lose focus and begin to aspire to higher levels of responsibility for the wrong motives. In the working world there is a phenomenon called the Peter Principle, wherein an individual is promoted one level beyond his or her capability. We have all seen it. An outstanding classroom instructor becomes an administrator and fails miserably because it is a position beyond his skill set or calling. An engineer, technically sound and well respected, ascends to a position of management and becomes frustrated with the distraction from her true interest in the nuts and bolts.

Many times financial gain is the motivator that causes one to seek greater responsibility. To be fair, this is more an indictment on some organizations' compensation systems than the individual's avarice. Some organizations, particularly the government sector, cannot statutorily compensate for performance beyond predetermined pay-grade boundaries. So some technicians who reach the top scale within their pay band aspire to management positions to increase their pay, even though they thoroughly enjoy their technical duties. Some people will go after any promotion that will increase their bottom line, often to the detriment of the organization and many times to the individuals themselves.

When we are told by others how invaluable we are, their praise sometimes takes root in our minds, and before long the idea is securely entrenched. Case in point: a friend of mine is a local gospel radio personality, and he disclosed to me that many times over the years he had been asked to serve as master of ceremony at various programs, sometimes on the same day with overlapping times. In many cases his ego was massaged by statements such as, "If you aren't there, the program won't be the same." He scurried from one event to the next because, after all, the very success of the program depended on his participation. All the while he convinced himself he was doing it for the Lord's glory. Later he admitted that he had an ego-driven need to be needed, and the fawning compliments and backslaps he received fed this need rather than exalting God. The enemy is cunning, and he gives us all the appropriate phrases to convince ourselves that our motives are pure. Deep inside we know this, but the allure of adulation and the charm of cajolery can be irresistible. The lie inherent in this form of seduction says that we are indispensable; in reality no one is. When I announced my retirement from the Department of Transportation, the job announcement soliciting a replacement was up within ten days.

Another reason for this insistence on taking on more duties is that sadly, for many, church is the only place they can assume responsibility, albeit sometimes without proper training. They lack skills and/or opportunity to wield any leadership in their professional lives and sometimes their own homes. So church ministry fills that void, that need to feel useful and, in some cases, important.

Whatever the reason, be it purpose, ego, or an outlet, when I observe this phenomenon of working for a cause to the detriment of other things, I recall my mother's advice. She drilled into her children that God has given us five senses and it behooves us to use them all. So whenever I feel that I'm doing a task out of *compunction* (sense of guilt) rather than *compulsion* (irresistible impulse), I recall her words of wisdom and make the appropriate decision. Her sage words have doubtless saved me a small fortune in stress-burnout therapy fees. As a result, I have learned to focus my efforts so that I can lead effectively, willingly, while maintaining a proper balance.

As we saw in chapter 1, it is possible to be fully aware of your calling and still shy away from it. Wavering can occur in one of two ways: (1) you can fail to believe God has uniquely assigned you to a certain work and consequently choose to run from your calling, or (2) you can respond to your calling but occasionally deviate and move into arenas that actually detract from your purpose. In imperative 1, I addressed the first waver tendency by suggesting that to rid your mind of the doubts surrounding your calling, you should adjust your auditory filter and trust your passion. The second waver tendency is more damaging because it reflects the majority of us who begin with the best of intentions and then permit circumstances to distract us from our stated purpose.

---

**How could a vision ever be given to someone to harbor if that person could not be trusted to carry it out. The message is simple: commitment precedes vision.**

*—High Eagle*

---

Televangelists are sometimes unfairly accused of building monuments to themselves under the guise of building God's kingdom. Yet the accusations resonate because it is simply counterintuitive to a lost world to see prominent clergy living in opulence and dressed in sartorial splendor while their sincere followers make extreme financial sacrifices to support the ministry. Granted, these high-profile ministers often came from humble beginnings and in some cases real poverty and deprivation. It is a credit to their hard work, commitment, vision, and God's blessing that they have attained their enviable status. They are to be commended for being industrious, but it is their extraordinary personal wealth that derails us and brings their credibility into question. They may whisper of humility and servitude with their lips, but their lifestyle screams of pomposity and privilege. The way they amass earthly mammon makes one think they intend to stay here indefinitely. Yet the old church hymn says:

I'm but a stranger here,
Heaven is my home;
Earth is a desert drear,
Heaven is my home;
There are the good and blest,
Those I loved most and best,
And there I, too, shall rest,
Heaven is my home.[1]

This modern-day preoccupation with accumulating wealth can be troubling to those who believe that the clergypersons who work daily to prepare us for the journey beyond these terrestrial shores sometimes conduct themselves as if they have no plans to make the trip. I have no doubt that most, if not all, of these anointed heralds of the gospel began their respective ministries with good intentions. Like John the Baptist, they simply desired to point others to the Savior. However, unlike John the Baptist, when they began to grow in stature, popularity, and prosperity, they lost focus, the antithesis of John's imperative to be focused. If they had only Jesus to imitate, they would find it easier to rationalize their shortcomings with a sanctified shrug that asks, "Well, who can truly match Jesus' example?" This is why I lift up John the Baptist, who represents the most common among us, as a model of effective leadership. Despite the masses that thronged to him and even believed him to be the reincarnated prophet Elijah, John remained focused and never succumbed to the fawning and adoration. He was faced with the same dilemma that popular evangelists are faced with, yet he demonstrated that it is possible to be anchored and unmoved by earthly treasure.

Moreover, Jesus himself, when standing before Pilate on the eve of his crucifixion, declared, "My kingdom is not of this world" (John 18:36). If one's view is truly heavenward, what purpose does accumulating inestimable wealth serve? If the answer is anything other than to use it to improve the human condition and demonstrate God's love, then the motives are misplaced. God prospers us so that we can assist others and set them on a course of self-sufficiency. Solomon, Job, Abraham, and many others were blessed by God with material wealth. I am not denouncing wealth. I am denouncing an improper motive for accumulating wealth. Christians should find it difficult to be smug in their affluence while others flounder and struggle to survive on meager wages.

Jesus' principles for managing money unfortunately have been lost over time. On April 8 and 9, 2007, CNN contributor and WVON-AM (Chicago) talk-show host Roland Martin hosted a televised CNN dialogue with clergy from various faiths titled "What Would Jesus Really Do?"[2] Several aspects of faith were examined, including prosperity and wealth. When asked his view, Pastor Rick Warren, author of the best seller *The Purpose Driven Life*, said, "Money is to be used and not loved. It is a tool. ... We're to love people and we're to use money. Now, what happens is if we start loving money, we end up using people to get it and we get the priorities reversed." Warren also said, "I don't think it's a sin to be rich. I think it's a sin to die rich." His point is that money is a tool to be used for good, not to be accumulated for personal gain and never recycled to help others.

Admittedly, most mega-ministries allocate considerable sums in their organizational budgets to help the poor and the bereft through various ministries to feed the hungry, clothe the naked, restore the addicted, and comfort the abused. But how many of them designate their personal resources to these same endeavors? Rick Warren reminded the audience that he and his wife "reverse tithe" and sustain themselves with 10 percent of their income while contributing 90 percent to ministry. I doubt there are many others who can make this claim. Let's do the math: If Rick Warren earned a mere dollar for every one of the 26 million books sold and retained 10 percent, that equates to 2.6 million pretax dollars with the remaining $23 million being sacrificially offered to elevate others through ministry. Most of us are selfish and would be very hard-pressed to follow Warren's example.

While televangelists are easy marks, the indictment of opulence can be levied against us all if we are content to live in our sumptuous havens while others are consigned to roll their Sisyphean burdens continuously uphill with no escape from their hellish existence.

When the young man asked Jesus, "Who is my neighbor?" he opened Pandora's box on our humane obligation to care for the least among us. We must renounce the world's advice to "look out for number one" and return to God's admonition to "love thy neighbor as thyself."

---

**Leaders aren't born—they are made. And they are made just like anything else, through hard work. And that's the price we'll have to pay to achieve that goal, or any goal.**

—*Vince Lombardi*

---

Local and national politicians are also susceptible to misplaced values, forgetting that people elect them to an office of honor to be their advocate and give voice to their concerns. Unfortunately, over time some become comfortable and acquire an entitlement mentality that they somehow deserve to retain their positions indefinitely, despite the scandalous behavior that we read about all too often in the daily news. If they do not have a mission statement or particular focus to keep them centered, then perhaps they should. Pride is insidious and cunning; it will take us down if we do not return to the touchstones that authenticate our purpose and intent.

## Rumble Strips

So how do we battle such a pernicious foe that seeks to keep us unfocused and ineffective? One tool available to everyone is a reasoned, purposefully worded mission statement. Like the rumble strips placed along the edges of interstate highways to alert drivers if they veer off the road, a mission statement can act as a rumble strip to help us stay on course. Admittedly, John the Baptist did not have a formal mission statement, but his mission was plain: to "bear witness of the Light, that all men through him might believe" (John 1:7).

Although John the Baptist did not couch his calling in terms such as *mission, focus,* and *purpose,* he certainly had a crystal clear sense of his role that precluded him from wandering into areas that did not contribute to his assigned work. John knew how critical it was that the Messiah's coming be foretold as prophesied. He knew that he was uniquely created to fulfill that mission. When you have no doubt that you are working within your true purpose, you will be excited and energized to give all you have to the task because you know it will eventually yield results.

Most organizations have a mission statement. However, most organizations do not do enough to keep the mission statement visible and ingrained in the minds of their members. A mission statement is generally developed as a component of an overall organizational strategic plan. After several hours, days, or weeks of development, the plan is printed, distributed, and shelved. Progressive organizations use the strategic plan as a compass; others may as well use it for compost, symbolic of yet another well-meaning product that ends up on the dung heap.

My advice is to rescue and extract the mission statement from the strategic plan and make it the guide for the organization's direction. And as with the rumble strips along the highway, whenever the organization delves into areas that do not square with its mission statement, it should experience an agitation to alert all that it is moving away from its intended focus. A well-worded mission statement will help sustain focus even if the organization's goals are not clearly articulated or staff members not properly trained. Note the following example.

At the church I attend, each ministry is required to develop a formal mission statement. This statement helps each ministry to get a grasp on imperative 1 concerning their calling, as well as remain true to that calling as imperative 2 emphasizes. Here is how it looks in practical terms. In most Missionary Baptist churches there are ushers and nurses who serve on the floor each Sunday. When "the Spirit is high" and a member is overcome with emotion or heat, it is the role of the nurse to come to this person's aid to ensure he or she is comforted, fanned, and resuscitated if necessary. Invariably during this moment of anxiety, an usher will offer assistance despite the nurse's presence. A precisely worded mission statement can help minimize disruption and clarify roles. For instance, in our church the ushers have a mission to *greet, seat, serve,* and *preserve.* The statement is embellished with other words to form a complete thought, but the primary action verbs form their mandate. So if someone needs a nurse, our ushers know that they are to serve the worshipper by knowing at all times where a nurse is stationed and seeing that the nurse is brought to the worshipper in a timely fashion. Anything beyond that is outside their role.

---

**Success consists of going from failure to failure without loss of enthusiasm.**

—*Winston Churchill*

---

In the absence of direct instruction or training, by simply following the tenets contained in the mission statement, ushers can use their own intuition and achieve success in greeting, seating, and serving parishioners while preserving the order and sanctity of the service.

## That's Church—What about the Real World?

The object lessons gleaned from crafting and employing a purposefully worded mission statement are not limited to the church and civic organizations. Profit-driven private industry companies must contend with these same issues. This is what makes John's seven leadership imperatives so effective: the concepts are transferable to all sectors of life.

In the African American community, barbershops and beauty salons serve as local meeting places. Aside from trading gossip, you can also obtain advice, political commentary, tickets to an upcoming concert, and lately, clothing. However, for these shops to remain vital, they must never forget their main purpose for existence is to provide a fresh cut and a stylish hairdo. If they ever begin focusing more on peddling than perming, their future as a hair salon is bleak.

To further the discussion of mission statements as they relate to purpose and focus, we need only take a quick review of two popular ones.

### BEN & JERRY'S ICE CREAM

The following is the mission statement of Ben & Jerry's ice cream: "To make, distribute & sell the finest quality all natural ice cream & euphoric concoctions with a continued commitment to incorporating wholesome, natural ingredients and promoting business practices that respect the Earth and the Environment."[3] Ben & Jerry's is recognized as an environmentally sensitive company, and that is reflected in their mission statement.

### GOOGLE

The Google mission statement reads: "To organize the world's information and make it universally accessible and useful."[4] I don't think anyone who has ever used the Google search engine would take exception to this stated mission. The goals and strategies that determine how they achieve the mission are dealt with internally. But in this statement the mission is clear to all employees and users.

## Who's Minding the Store?

Even the best companies have occasionally failed to heed the rumble strip and in turn moved away from their core business, resulting in severe customer and profit loss. Following are a few examples.

During the mid-1980s, when gas prices were high, General Motors made a decision to downsize its traditionally long, massive Cadillac sedan with a design that approximated the other GM product line. In fact, they were almost indiscernible. The Cadillac resembled certain Buicks, Pontiacs, Chevrolets, and Oldsmobiles. Predictably, customers accustomed to their symbol of success revolted and voted with their protests and their pocketbooks. Failure to listen to its customer base cost GM dearly. Nevertheless, GM adjusted as soon as it could, and today it is still producing the very luxurious and distinctive trademark Cadillac sedan.

Another corporate example of the perils of losing focus is Coca-Cola's introduction of a new formula in 1985. The change in this classic beverage caused a tremendous uproar from loyal Coke drinkers. Many of them stockpiled as much of the traditional Coke as they could find, refusing to switch to the new and improved version. It was not long before Coca-Cola relented and brought back the original cola under the name "Coke Classic."

My final example is the Krispy Kreme donut company. This North Carolina–based company existed since 1937 under the radar and was available mostly in the Southern states and the District of Columbia. If you have ever visited a Krispy Kreme store and witnessed the donuts moving along the conveyor, each one doused with a heavy amount of gooey glaze, then flipped over and deftly placed into a box by an attendant, you know there is nothing that compares.

In April 2000 Krispy Kreme went public at twenty-one dollars per share and reached a high share price of about fifty dollars. But by December 2006 stock prices were hovering around ten dollars per share. What happened? Kate O'Sullivan of *CFO Magazine* provided an insightful and thorough analysis in a June 1, 2005, article.[5] Krispy Kreme had been a small-town business since its inception. Once this Southern gem was unearthed, it began to grow in popularity. Rapid growth contributed to its decline, but more so, I believe it was rapid expansion and exposure. Krispy Kreme's trademark and uniqueness was their hot-off-the-assembly-line donuts. When the company went public in 2000, investors pressured for more exposure and saturation. Therefore the donuts began to surface everywhere in prepackaged form, far removed from their core presentation. Why would a company deviate from the thing that made it unique and branded it in an already crowded market? Jonathan Waite, an analyst for KeyBanc Capital Markets in Los Angeles, expressed the problem, saying, "They [Krispy Kreme] need to emphasize the hot-doughnut experience, rather than the cold, old doughnut in a gas station."[6]

---

**I have not failed. I've just found 10,000 ways that won't work.**

*—Thomas Alva Edison*

---

When I coached girls' recreational league basketball, I told the taller girls to always hold the rebound high above their heads and *never* bring their hands down to the height level of the shorter opponents. I told them if they aren't going to take advantage of their God-given advantage, they may as well not have it. The same advice applies to any organization with a proven niche and competitive advantage. To succumb to anything that takes you away from your core could prove to be very damaging, sometimes irreparably so.

## No One Is Immune

Have you seen a local pastor who is so involved in every worthy cause in the community that he or she rarely has time or strength to minister to the primary pastoral calling? Such pastors are well meaning and sincere, but unfortunately, they have lost his way along the trail. I know of one pastor who, to his credit, resigned from pastoral ministry and became a full-time evangelist rather than spend so much time away from his congregation. He recognized that he was better suited to evangelize than to pastor.

While I believe this loss of focus can occur when a pastor becomes embroiled in other activities outside of his or her calling, I acknowledge up front that the church has produced some extraordinary political and civic leaders. In fact, it is the financial independence afforded to them by a church that permits pastors to boldly declare their convictions without fear of retaliation. Were it not for the church, Martin Luther King Jr. and other civil rights preachers would have been silenced. Nevertheless, when the winds of fortune create a crisis that force a choice between effective service to the local call and a call to serve the masses, one should pray mightily for guidance. Rare is the individual who can lead country, community, and congregation concurrently.

The story is told of a little boy who was left in a field by his father and told to pull weeds until he returned. Later a car pulled up with two men who were lost and trying to find their way to town. They asked the little boy for directions. He said, "Town is that way," pointing to his right. As the men walked back to their car, the boy said, "Wait, town is that way," pointing to his left. The two men became exasperated and scolded the boy.

"Son, you don't know anything! You don't know how to get to town and you don't even know where you are!" The boy replied, "Oh, I know where I am—I'm right where my father placed me." It is a simple story but profound. Once you know where you have been divinely appointed to contribute to society, stay there until you receive further instructions.

As most children do, I loved watching cartoons growing up. One of my favorite cartoons was very instructive and I believe applicable to our discussion here. Those of you born before 1990 may recall a cartoon involving Mr. Wizard the Lizard and his protégé Tooter the Turtle. In each episode Tooter would come to Mr. Wizard expressing a desire to become someone exciting, such as a firefighter, mountain climber, astronaut, or jungle explorer. Mr. Wizard would wave his magic wand and transport Tooter to a place where he could live out his fantasy. Invariably Tooter would get into a calamitous situation and begin crying out, "Help, Mr. Wizard!" Mr. Wizard would chant these words in his heavy German dialect, "Drizzle, drazzle, druzzle, drome, time for this one to come home," rescuing Tooter and returning him safely home. After Tooter vowed that he would never again seek to be anything other than what he was created to be, the Wizard would end with the admonition, "Be what you are, not what you are not; those who do this are the happiest lot." Not bad for a cartoon, huh? The moral is timeless and relevant: *Be focused* in your calling and purpose.

In the entire region during his time and just before Jesus began his earthly ministry, John the Baptist was the most well-known man yet was unpopular among the religious leaders. Four hundred years had passed since God had spoken through a bona fide prophet, and the people were starving for an inspired word. John delivered his message, and regardless of the fame (or notoriety) it brought him, he remained resolute in his call and mission. Imperative 3 will explore John's humble approach to his controversial and polarizing vocation.

## Points to Consider

**1.** How essential is it to remain focused on your calling or life purpose?

**2.** Can you recall a time that a mission statement did help or would have helped your organization or ministry remain focused?

**3.** When have you felt overcommitted? How did you resolve it?

**4.** Why do you feel most people take on multiple tasks?

**5.** Is it ever justifiable to neglect your family and place them secondary to your mission?

**6.** Whom do you personally know who exemplifies imperative 2, "Be focused"?

**7.** How would your life to this point have been different if you had applied this imperative?

# Humble

He it is, who coming after me is preferred before me, whose shoe's latches I am not worthy to unloose.

—JOHN 1:27

In imperatives 1 and 2 we learned from John the Baptist the importance of being diligent in determining our purpose and then, having discovered it, remaining focused and resolute. These two imperatives alone can be life changing if applied daily. Going through life aimlessly, hit-or-miss, perhaps achieving some degree of success but never really being engaged in the thing that you were uniquely created to do, creates a restless sense of unfinished business. That is why some people, even after attaining stardom, feel empty and unfulfilled. Success in a particular area does not necessarily mean that you are operating in your preordained place.

Others know in what areas they are supposed to function, but they allow things to distract them. Some are equipped with the ability to do more than one thing quite effectively; others are not. The latter individuals, prone to delve into activities that compete for their attention, will soon discover that their lack of focus has been detrimental. Although purpose and focus are vital, still there is more to becoming an effective leader. A focused and purposeful leader can be effective, but even more so if a humble disposition is developed and maintained. An individual must *be humble* in her aspirations for leadership and then, having attained that position, *be humble* in carrying out her charge.

Contrary to conventional wisdom, leaders do not leap forward; they are pushed forward. I can recall as early as elementary school that when it came time to choose sides for a game, the same guys invariably were selected by the rest of us to be team captains and do the selecting. Not once do I recall either of the captains demanding this privilege; and rarely do I recall anyone challenging them for this role. True leaders exude confidence, and the confidence of others is bestowed upon them without solicitation. Some might characterize them as "born leaders."

I also noticed that there was an understood pecking order. If the usual boys were not participating, other captains were volunteered through this same process of tacit democracy. Most shied away from this burden of responsibility, but those assembled intuitively knew who among us was most capable of leadership. I discovered that boys who pushed their way to power often repelled those expected to follow them.

---

**Good leaders must first become good servants.**
*—Robert Greenleaf*

---

Leadership is not something to be sought for personal gain but something thrust upon an individual by necessity. Any sane vice president of the United States, although willing at a moment's notice to fill the president's seat, has no desire to supplant or replace the president and take on all the responsibility that comes with the position. This is not to suggest that some have not eagerly awaited their turn to serve, but they are wise to wait for the appropriate time—the next election!

John the Baptist did not vainly pursue his role as a forerunner, but was chosen at birth. He was thrust onto the stage of history because of his suitability as an obedient and humble vessel. His focus was on a liberating Lord rather than his own looming legacy. Consequently, Jesus himself was moved to say of John, "Assuredly, I say to you, among those born of women there has not risen one greater than John the Baptist" (Matthew 11:11, NKJV). What an endorsement and affirmation of God's requirement of humility over haughtiness!

A twentieth-century example of a selfless and unassuming leader who illustrates my contention that leaders are pushed forward is Dr. Martin Luther King Jr. Led by the power of God, he made tremendous strides in the march toward freedom and equality for all people. Despite having lived only thirty-nine years, his impact on society and world consciousness is remarkable. Moreover, the record reflects that he did not seek prominence, but rather that he was thrust into leadership during an impromptu rally organized in response to the unfair treatment of a seamstress named Rosa Parks. Many times during this young man's life, he questioned his ability to lead such an awesome movement for racial justice.

---

**I believe the first test of a truly great man [sic] is his humility.**

*—John Ruskin*

---

In *Martin & Malcolm & America*, Dr. James H. Cone records that Andrew Young, a King protégé, insisted that "Martin did not ambitiously pursue leadership. I'm convinced he never wanted to be a leader. I mean, everything he did, he was pushed into." Young went on the say that King "got trapped into the Montgomery Improvement Association," the organization that coordinated the year-long bus boycott.[1] Throughout King's time of leadership, he always considered and many times deferred to the preestablished civil rights giants, such as Roy

Wilkins (NAACP) and A. Philip Randolph (Brotherhood of Sleeping Car Porters). Although he was gaining the headlines and making appearances on *Meet the Press* and other prominent venues, he was always careful to consider the implications of his actions as they related to the NAACP and other organizations. He never felt that he was the hub around which the spokes turned. In his mind he was just one spoke on the proverbial wheel of justice and equality. Even though King had detractors from within and without, King understood his mission and focus and humbly regarded the contributions of all who joined in the mutual struggle.

John's actions of preaching and warning others about the coming Messiah evoked a visit and inquiry from the Sanhedrin representatives, the highest ruling religious authority among the Jews. Yet John never allowed the attention to go to his head, but simply declared his unworthiness even to untie the sandal strings from the dusty feet of the coming Messiah (John 1:27). Not only was John sure of his calling, but he remained focused and humble.

Be very wary of individuals who crave positions of leadership and authority. They may have usable skills but are most likely emotionally immature. Positions of authority appear glamorous and exciting, but those who hold these positions will tell you that they are often lonely, misunderstood, abandoned, questioned, challenged, attacked, and undermined. The adages "No guts, no glory"; "No pain, no gain"; and "No cross, no crown" all hold true. Jesus himself had to put two of his own disciples, James and John, in check when they sought a promise of prominence in his coming kingdom. He rebuked them with a challenge, asking, "Are you able to drink the cup that I am about to drink?" (Matthew 20:22, NKJV). Leadership looks glittery because of the homage we pay to our leaders, but don't be deceived: life exacts a severe cost for the privilege of serving others.

In 2005 Indianapolis Colts coach Tony Dungy lost his son to suicide despite having raised him in a loving Christian home.

Dungy, spokesman for the family-betterment group All Pro Dads, cannot be blamed for this tragedy, but his demanding job as an NFL coach does involve a tremendous sacrifice of time away from his family. In 2007 Philadelphia Eagles coach Andy Reid requested a leave of absence at the conclusion of the season to attend to the unlawful and aberrant behavior of his two sons. Like Dungy, Reid sacrificed countless hours away from his family, and despite his best efforts when he *was* around, calamity occurred. Unfortunately, many successful professionals, from coaches to pastors to CEOs, invest considerable hours of time in their "teams," and sometimes their own spouses and children are neglected and resentful. Indeed, it is a twisted sort of irony that our zeal in pursuing our calling sometimes threatens the families who are an integral part of our life's mission. The outcome is incongruous with the intention.

The stress of leadership is telling in the change in appearance of the president of the United States after serving a term or two in office. The sacrifices the president makes and the weightiness of daily decisions manifest themselves in physical changes, such as dark circles around the eyes, thinner and sometimes grayer hair, and pronounced facial wrinkles. Other public figures, such as civil rights leader Martin Luther King Jr. and black nationalist Malcolm X gave their lives trying to improve the conditions for blacks and others; tragically, both were murdered at age thirty-nine.

---

**I long to accomplish a great and noble task, but it is my chief duty to accomplish humble tasks as though they were great and noble.**

*—Helen Keller*

---

Who among us would not be flattered to have a postage stamp issued bearing our image? But are we willing to live a life of self-denial and service to be so honored? Similarly, when we see others prospering, we admire what they have, often wishing we were as fortunate. I chuckle when I recall making a comment to a friend about desiring to live a life of retirement much like that enjoyed by his older brother. My friend replied, "That's fine, but are you also willing to work a three-job, twenty-hour workday for nearly thirty years?" Having had it put to me that way, I hurriedly retracted my statement!

While most of us do not covet the responsibility that comes with the mantle of leadership, we all long for some level of recognition. Even an infant will cry and demand validation of his or her expressed needs. One way to gain affirmation of worth is to hold a position of authority whereby we can influence others and mobilize them in a way that is successful and fulfilling. To personally steer a project from concept to completion is exhilarating and ego gratifying; our ego is fed to the point that we feel good about our achievement without feeling pompous. In the final analysis, we all would like to believe that our being here matters, that we count for something. The most discouraging reality for most of us would be to live and die and have no one ever take note of our existence—or our exit.

This desire to be regarded as someone of value is often evident in the church, where an implied importance goes along with being in a position of leadership. Even though you may not have earned a high school diploma, in the church you are able to appropriate respect because of your office. Church workers are not always required to have formal leadership training or skills; the major requirements often are availability and commitment. Some manage to lead very well, others less so. Nevertheless, the need for acknowledgment of self-worth is strong and can lead to an ill-advised quest for responsibility beyond one's capability. The example of John the Baptist is this: he captivates the attention of the world and is in a position to exploit it for maximum personal gain, yet he remains focused and, above all else, humbly eschews any undue adulation.

John models the principle of Romans 12:3 that we are not to think of ourselves more highly than we ought to. Note that this verse does not say to think of ourselves as lowly; nor does it say not to think of ourselves in a healthy manner. Rather, we are to maintain balance and not think of ourselves "more highly" than we ought. I have known people to get elected to public office and then forget all about their old friends. When they become "The Honorable," they no longer treat old friends with the same affection or regard. They take on a self-importance that demeans the very ones they were elected to serve. Their lives become more about being powerful and less about serving the powerless.

## The Dynamics of Leadership

Before moving on to discuss in detail the notion of humble leadership, I need to provide a few thoughts about the dynamics of leadership. Emerging events demand that a leader be found to respond to the issue at hand, and usually the selected leader does not seek the responsibility. Rather, those expected to follow will recognize a person's abilities and conscript that person into service. Even politicians, though they may covertly consider an office, will form an exploratory committee to gauge public support before announcing their candidacy. They are usually motivated by a culmination of others' repeated murmurings about their electability to office. Before taking exception to my assertion that leaders are pushed forward, recall that I am referring to persons of good character who are unassuming, levelheaded, and not overly ambitious.

Leadership is best understood in an analysis of team or group dynamics. In every group or team, a leader is appointed to facilitate the accomplishment of a task. If effective, the leader will be organized, open-minded, focused, fair, and receptive to differing viewpoints. These attributes forge team loyalty and respect for the leader. When the official leader lacks these attributes, the team members instinctively and without collaboration identify the informal leader and look to that person for direction and validation. The informal leader has the benefit of the team's confidence and fills the void while being careful not to undermine the official group leader's authority. At critical junctures in meetings, someone will invariably turn to the informal leader and say, "What do you think is our best course of action?" Others will permit the discussion to meander until the informal leader offers his or her reasoned opinion. Either way, the team defers to this person's perspective before taking action because of the confidence they have placed in his or her judgment.

Another by-product of effective team leadership is that when a team is in sync and producing results, a contagious surge of energy exists, resulting in the rotating of leadership. As different skill sets are required, the team member with the appropriate skills will emerge to lead the effort. This is best observed with athletic teams. In a game of basketball, if the inside low-post game is restricted by the defenders, the responsibility falls on the shooters to make their jump shots. The responsibility for the team's success rotates from the post players to the perimeter shooters.

---

**Leaders are more powerful role models when they learn than when they teach.**

*—Rosabeth Moss Kantor*

---

Effective team leaders delegate responsibility appropriately rather than holding to the old adage "If you want something done right, do it yourself." This philosophy will carry a leader for a while, but it is unsustainable as more demands are made of the leader. It is better to train and trust others than to retain and drain yourself! When a leader refuses to delegate, the members are relegated to the role of ineffectual bystanders without a vested interest in the outcome of the team's success. The members don't mature and develop, and the project outcome may be inadequate due to the lack of input from the team members. In this context I concur with the lighthearted adage "Two heads are better than one, even if the other is only a head of cabbage!"

## The Source of True Humility

Since John the Baptist commands that we seek humility, how do we cultivate this critical characteristic? Humility is a character trait that only God can impart. Or to say it another way, when you fully recognize the superiority of the only true celestial power that is higher than yourself, your smallness in the universe becomes glaring and you become grateful for the opportunity to be used in a divine plan that transcends personal will or ambition. Many times a lack of spiritual grounding can cause lapses in judgment among leaders. When corporate magnates misappropriate gargantuan sums of money, resulting in the destruction of companies, they have plainly lost connection with the One who never sleeps or slumbers and sees more than we do.

Need I add that corporate magnates are not the only ones guilty of ethics lapses? Many religious leaders, both prominent and obscure, both mega and meager, sometimes swerve from their courses due to the mind-altering sins of pride and avarice. The words of another John, the beloved disciple, caution, "Do not love the world or the things in the world. . . . For all that *is* in the world—the lust of the flesh, the lust of the eyes, and the pride of life—is not of the Father but is of the world" (1 John 2:15-16, NKJV). When anyone in secular or religious service focuses on the temporal bounty of life, he or she is a candidate for self-destruction. Of the more than one hundred warnings in the Bible against pride, arguably the most known is "Pride goeth before destruction, and an haughty spirit before a fall" (Proverbs 16:18).

Humility is a character trait that eludes many as they began to believe their own press or trust solely in their own abilities. They become obsessed with their reputation and stature and through various machinations seek to establish themselves supreme over others.

Dr. Cleophus LaRue, professor of preaching and worship at Princeton University, delivered a sermon titled "How to Make a Name for Yourself."[2] LaRue's text was Philippians 2:5-10. In this letter to the Philippians, the apostle Paul was writing to the first congregation he organized in Europe. He was so extremely fond of these people that his letter is colloquially referred to as his love letter to the Philippians. LaRue pointed out that Paul didn't have much to criticize this congregation for except for one subtle trend he began detecting. The city of Philippi was named for King Phillip II (who would eventually have a son known in history as Alexander the Great), and consequently, some of the citizens of this city had a huge ego problem. Paul saw the pride common to the city creeping into the infant church as everyone jockeyed for prestige and prominence. Paul reminded them that a leader is most of all a sacrificing servant, relying on God to do the elevating. Paul admonished them to "let this mind be in you, which was also in Christ Jesus" (2:5). Christ, the co-creator of the universe came to earth in the form of a man for the express purpose of dying an atoning death for fallen humankind. He was willing to die in the cruelest and most disgraceful form of death for a Jew, being hung on a cross. He humbled himself and submitted to this despicable display of degradation.

LaRue insightfully noted in the sermon that everyone wants to be a big shot. He said, "People just want to be 'big'; you can even call them a dog as long as you call them a 'big dog'!" He concluded the sermon with the reminder that the only true way to earn a name of noteworthiness is to submit as Christ did and let God elevate you. "Therefore God also has highly exalted Him and given Him the name which is above every name, that at the name Jesus every knee should bow, of those in heaven, and of those on earth, and of those under the earth" (Philippians 2:9-10, NKJV).

As a leader in the local church or elsewhere, you will have times when you will have to back down from some stances, even when you are on solid footing. If you remain humble and steadfast in what you have been ordained to do, God will reward you in surprising ways.

A humble leader is able to take a broad view, realizing that the achievement of the task far exceeds the accolades that follow. At times others will either take credit or be given credit for something you may have achieved or initiated. If any earthly credit is to be given, you certainly deserve it. However, we don't have to live much beyond grade school age to learn that life is not always fair. We simply have to remain humble, realizing as my former pastor Rev. Wilfred McKinley used to intone, "The cause of Christ is greater than all of us!"[3] With this as a mantra, it is much easier to work within your calling focused and humble.

> You do not lead by hitting people over the head—that's assault, not leadership.
>
> —*Dwight D. Eisenhower*

John the Baptist possessed this God-given characteristic of humility. He was mistaken by many as the coming Messiah at a time when people were thirsting for such an appearance. He could have succumbed to the temptation to bask in the adoration and attention. He could have exacted some material gain from the gullible and well-meaning congregants. He could have played the hand that was dealt and portrayed himself as the one they believed him to be.

I recall the movie *Coming to America* with Eddie Murphy and Arsenio Hall. In one scene a young lady believes Simi, played by Hall, to be the crowned prince of Zumunda, when in actuality the prince is Hakeem, played by Murphy. Rather than be truthful, Simi permits her to believe erroneously that he is the prince. John the Baptist, however, did no such thing. Instead, he kept his focus as the forerunner of the Messiah, humbly accepting his role and performing it to the best of his ability, despite how much others unwittingly sought to distract him. When asked if he was the long-awaited Messiah, John said that not only was he not the Messiah, but that he wasn't even worthy to remove the sandals from the Messiah's dusty, aching feet. Imagine how John could have exploited the situation. Imagine how some do today.

## No One Succeeds Alone

The challenge for anyone aspiring to leadership is to maintain a humble disposition, affirming English poet John Donne's reflection that "no man is an island, entire of itself; every man is a piece of the continent, a part of the main." No leader ever achieved anything without the support of others. To act otherwise is to marginalize those who willingly offer their allegiance and trust. The late Sam Walton, Wal-Mart founder, coined the company slogan that persists today: "Our people make the difference." Wal-Mart is among many companies that extol the worth of its employees, often referring to them as "our most valuable company asset." The most effective leaders recognize that nothing gets accomplished without a competent, motivated, and trained workforce. A leader who neglects to invest in his people, whether employees or volunteers, may have some short-term success, but there is no foundational endurance. They will have built a wide organization with no depth. The lasting organizations drill deep, not superficially wide.

Ineffective leaders are power-centered, territorial, selfish, uncaring, and headline grabbing. Nothing demoralizes esprit de corps more than hearing the leader taking credit for all the successes and sidestepping all the failures. Even in sports we despise this behavior. Former Philadelphia Eagles wide receiver Terrell Owens is a sure bet for the Hall of Fame if his performance remains constant. Although he is respected for his production, he is equally disliked for his tendency to hang his teammates out to dry when the team play suffers. He is not above labeling his teammates as noncompetitive and holding himself up as the only one making a meaningful contribution. His stock among the fans hit rock bottom when he maligned the beloved team leader and quarterback Donovan McNabb. If he had reviewed recent sports history, he would have known that wide receiver Jerry Rice was as highly esteemed as quarterback Joe Montana of the San Francisco 49ers because of his unselfishness and appreciation for the efforts of his teammates. Owens had the potential to be equally revered as a team leader, but he blew it by taking undue credit for the team's success and dispensing undue blame for its failures.

---

**If I have seen farther than others, it is because I was standing on the shoulders of giants.**

*—Isaac Newton*

---

The late Dr. E. V. Hill, former pastor of Mount Zion Baptist Church in Los Angeles, preached a profound and memorable sermon titled "Joseph's Seat" at an Evangel Temple Ministers' Conference in Baltimore.[4] He said that while it may be tempting to covet Joseph's seat as second only to that of Pharaoh, remember that to sit in that seat Joseph endured rejection by his brothers, enslavement to traders, false accusations by his master's wife, unjust incarceration, and abandonment by a fellow inmate. To sit in Joseph's seat requires (1) an unwavering belief that you are part of a divine plan and (2) a spirit of humility that compels you to serve faithfully no matter what your circumstances or challenges.

## Humility Is Not Timidity

Oscar Wilde once said, "Life imitates art far more than art imitates life." However, when art *does* imitate life, it can be very instructional. When I think of humility, I recall the television series *Kung Fu* starring David Carradine as Kwai Chang Caine. This Eastern-influenced Western captured my imagination. It was fascinating to watch the young grasshopper's emergence from a fledgling to a full-blown Shaolin priest. In each episode we learned more about his intensive training and all the life lessons taught to him by his mentors. His most prevalent characteristic was his humility. Even though he was capable of subduing any assailants, his first instinct was to avoid conflict, or at least to avoid conflict until circumstances gave him the advantage. Caine was not timid; he was humble. He was not a coward; he was a warrior with control.

John the Baptist likewise was not timid. Recall that when the religious authorities came to the river to determine John's identity, he reproached them, calling them a "brood of vipers" (Matthew 3:7, NKJV). A coward never would have dared called the ranking religious party such a derisive name. Even though he was humble enough to know his place in God's plan, he was also bold enough to speak his mind and expose insincerity wherever it resided.

## Confidence Is Not Arrogance

The scene opens with a tall, handsome, dark-skinned man dressed in a natty business suit disembarking from a train ride from Philadelphia, Pennsylvania, to Sparta, Mississippi. His purpose is to investigate a suspicious murder. You may recall the actor as Sidney Poitier and the movie as the Academy Award–winning *In the Heat of the Night,* a 1967 thriller that explored the racial tensions of that era. In one memorable scene Poitier interviews a local citizen at his spacious mansion, complete with "Negro" servants. During the intense questioning, the white Southerner maliciously slaps Poitier in the face for his "insolence." Without hesitating, Poitier responds in kind with a startling and unprecedented backhanded slap to the man's face. This educated, experienced, assured, and competent black man, although respectful and professional, was by no means weak and cowardly. Humility and self-confidence are not incompatible attributes. John the Baptist also exuded confidence without being arrogant. I am sure the people were stunned by the way he addressed the religious leaders. John gave voice to what others could only mutter under their breath about the religious leaders.

> **Consult your friend on all things, especially on those which respect yourself. His counsel may then be useful where your own self-love might impair your judgment.**
>
> *—Seneca*

It is particularly important that we recognize that John the Baptist was no pansy! He didn't flinch from conflict or action. He was principled, and he was courageous. Many times when we speak of humility in the church realm, soothing instruments can be heard in the background lulling us into an idyllic stupor. We are admonished to "turn the other cheek" and rarely are encouraged to "speak truth to power." For too long we have promoted a serene and pastoral image of church, and the rugged thrill seekers—men especially but also strong women—have simply opted out. We must highlight the audacity of biblical role models such as John the Baptist. We must give people permission to be strong—to challenge, explore, and conquer. We have to let them see the true character of our scriptural ancestors in faith, not watered-down, pacifying versions. When we stop asking men to check their masculinity at the visitor's center and demanding that women surrender their leadership skills at the sanctuary door, we will see people of all personalities and backgrounds spilling over into the pews, ready to assume positions of leadership with strength *and* humility.

John had such an impact on people that some desired to become his disciples. They saw in him a man led by God, full of conviction, integrity, courage, and vision. In the final analysis, that is what most people look for in their leaders. Leaders don't have to have all the answers, but they must convey a sense of purpose and unwavering resolve to the issue at hand. If you are in a leadership position, be sure of your goal, remain focused, walk humbly among your followers, and be alert to shifting conditions. With imperative 4, "Be discerning," we will observe the insightful awareness of this untrained wilderness preacher as he walked in his purpose.

## Points to Consider

**1.** How essential is it to remain humble as you lead others?

**2.** Do you believe there can be informal leaders? Give examples.

**3.** What kinds of things make if difficult to remain humble as a leader?

**4.** How can you be both humble and outspoken?

**5.** Does the church promote a welcoming environment for both women and men? If so, describe how.

**6.** Whom do you know personally who exemplifies imperative 3, "Be humble"?

**7.** How would your life to this point have been different if you had applied this imperative?

# BE Discerning

The next day John seeth Jesus coming unto
him, and saith, Behold the Lamb of God, which
taketh away the sin of the world.

—JOHN 1:29

In the preceding chapter we saw how essential it is for leaders to demonstrate humility when carrying out their duties. We also determined that leadership is not something to be gained through connivance, subversion, self-promotion, or other manifestations of overzealous ambition. Real leadership is willingly bestowed by those who have observed and drawn strength from the confidence that exudes naturally from a person. The Sanhedrin rulers of John's day may have been the official leaders of the Jewish community, but it was John who captured the imagination of the people and drew them in droves to his riverside rostrum. The people proclaimed John as the genuine oracle of God. Yet despite this unsolicited attention and deference, while dispensing his duties, John remained vigilant and watchful for the physical appearance and revelation that would authenticate and conclude his ministry. From antiquity he adjures us to *be discerning*.

## How Long, Lord?

Have you as a leader ever waited on God to show some sign that you were headed the right direction or that the events swirling around you were somehow still in God's divine plan? The most difficult part of leadership is waiting on God to move. The common cry is "How long, Lord?" I believe that God sometimes gives leaders confirmation, but they fail to recognize it. To see God moving in your situation requires a discerning view of your landscape. By "discerning" I mean an intentional observation of events occurring around you, watchful for an opportunity or indicator that the anticipated breakthrough is imminent. Of course, once seeing the opportunity, discernment requires you to take action. I had a boss who used to call it "reading the tea leaves." My uneducated father used a practical analogy that adds even more light to the notion of intentional observation or discernment.

I have never farmed, but both my parents were raised on farms in the Carolinas. My father used to regale me with stories of his childhood life as a sharecropper, farming land owned by another for a portion of the proceeds generated by the season's harvest. One thing he told me is that it is very possible to plow with your head down, but it will likely result in a crooked furrow. A good plow hand looks out ahead with one eye on the mark to ensure a straight furrow. By keeping his head up, he also spots obstacles that lie ahead. Like the plow hand, a good leader must move forward with head raised, navigating around obstacles and making adjustments while remaining focused on the goal.

Discernment is not to be confused with possessing vision. Not everyone is visionary and able to see far in advance of realization those things that can be achieved. Vision is generally the responsibility of the official leader of the organization. It is his or her obligation to conceive, communicate, and build a coalition of support for the fulfillment of the vision. In the church, the task of providing the vision or "future look" of the church is similarly assigned to the leadership—to the pastor who is supported by the lay leaders. Likewise, in the corporate setting, the CEO conceives and communicates the vision for the "future look" of the company, supported by the board of directors. The CEO may arrive at the vision with input from other key executives, but the final articulation of the vision rests on that CEO's shoulders. Although everyone is not privy to the vision, all of us can be discerning, as demonstrated by this "everyman," John the Baptist.

The Bible records that John was at the river preaching one message: "Repent . . . for the kingdom of heaven is at hand" (Matthew 3:2). How long he had preached this message is unknown, but we know by the reaction of the crowds that it was effective and compelling. John the Baptist had been warning of the coming Messiah, and one day as Jesus approached, he exclaimed, "Behold the Lamb of God, which taketh away the sin of the world" (John 1:29). He divulged to those who followed him that he too had been unaware of the Messiah's identity but realized that it was required of him to baptize with water if the Messiah was to be made known to Israel (v. 31). John reports that when he baptized Jesus he saw the Spirit descend from heaven like a dove and remain on Jesus. This, he recalled, was the sign that was given to him by God to let him know that the Messiah had emerged (vv. 32-33).

---

**I shall light a candle of understanding in thine heart, which shall not be put out.**

—*2 Esdras 14:25, in the Apocrypha*

---

It is interesting that John, who surely must have known Jesus, the son of Joseph and Cousin Mary, never saw him as anyone other than a carpenter's son until that day at the riverside. Isn't it hard to fathom that, apparently, his mother never told him of his own miraculous conception and his father's temporary inability to speak (Luke 1:13-20), given their tradition of transmitting history orally? It is equally hard to imagine that John was not told how he had leaped in his mother's womb when the highly favored Cousin Mary entered his mother's home. It was such a significant moment that his mother, Elizabeth, blessed Mary, causing Mary to joyously offer a prayer of thanks (vv. 41-55).

Yet it was not until that specific day and time when Jesus came to the river to be baptized by John that John finally recognized Jesus as the Messiah. This suggests that God may withhold the revelation of his true intent and purpose for your life until a divinely appointed time. Even some PKs (preacher's kids) who were destined to follow their father or mother into ordained ministry would tell you that they had no idea when that moment would occur. Some were more resistant than others and tried a different path before coming full circle to the calling placed on them at birth. This could account for John's declaration that he himself had been unaware of the Messiah's identity.

Ironically, preachers today are subject to what I call "convenient familiarity." To those who have no interest in the formal church, the preacher is "just a human being" who is no more connected to God than anyone else. Some even go so far as to label the preacher a pimp, a thief, or an opportunist. To be sure, just as one can find politicians, CEOs, educators, businesspersons, attorneys, and people in other professions with questionable motives, one can find "suspect" clergy as well. Yet when dire circumstances befall the person with a cynical veneer, that previously maligned preacher is summoned to offer solace, supplication, or service. Although the preacher is subject to the same human flaws that afflict and challenge everyone, when it is time to relay God's direction to the people, that man or woman can be transformed into an instrument in God's hand.

## Discernment in Action

Through John's example we see the importance of being discerning and in touch with events around us, recognizing clues and early indicators. How does this awareness play out in reality? If your church is located in an area that is becoming populated with immigrants, are you expressing disgust and resentment or are you mobilizing to provide an environment that is welcoming and inclusive? Are you actively seeking a person with bilingual skills to join your staff? If your church is located in an area slated for redevelopment, are you organizing a community-development corporation so that you become eligible for funding that allows you to become a participant in the revitalization rather than a casualty? If your church is experiencing the deterioration of marriages at an unusual rate, are you responding with trained, professional intervention, or are you content with helping both parties prepare for life postdivorce? If your church has an inordinate number of families experiencing financial duress, are you establishing a process to aid them in long-term financial planning, or are you absolving your conscience by offering an occasional workshop, even though it will be ineffective without consistent assistance and monitoring? If your church is feeling the effects of drug and gun violence, is your church confronting the aberrant behavior, or is it resigned to wait for the inevitable funerals rather than stop the carnage and suffering at its source? Is your church actively engaged in holding those in governmental positions of power accountable to God's moral standard, or is your stance that soteriology alone is the church's purpose and mission?

Many churches are attuned to events affecting their congregants and their community and are gamely attacking these prickly issues. To some, what I speak of smacks of the conviction that the church has to have a social gospel if it is to be relevant. Others would disagree and say that Jesus' great commission commands the church to "teach all nations, baptizing them in the name of the Father, and of the Son, and of the Holy Ghost" (Matthew 28:19). I believe that Jesus' commission encompassed both perspectives, for he continues in verse 20, "teaching them to observe all things whatsoever I have commanded you." Did not his teachings include a regard for humanity and speak of civil justice and of compassion and love for the least among us? Did not his teachings speak of fiscal stewardship, appropriate behavior, and effective parenting? Did not his teachings address all aspects of the human condition? John's command to be discerning is a call for spiritual sobriety and unflinching courage.

During CNN contributor and talk-show host Roland Martin's televised dialogue with clergy from various faiths titled "What Would Jesus Really Do?" one of the invited clergy was emphatic that if Jesus were physically present today, he would be found hanging out with and ministering to those infected with HIV/AIDS or in bondage to drugs and alcohol. Rev. Frederick D. Haynes III, senior pastor of Friendship West Baptist Church in Dallas, said that "Jesus would be right there with us, uniting in holy wedlock, salvation and liberation for community transformation."[1]

In times of change, learners inherit the Earth, while the learned find themselves beautifully equipped to deal with a world that no longer exists.

—*Eric Hoffer*

This principle translates to you as the leader of your particular ministry or organization in much the same fashion as it pertains to a pastor or senior leader. If you are responsible for community outreach, do you have a mechanism in place to keep you abreast of the things impacting your community? Are you listening and looking for recurring problems that indicate a trend? If many potential converts have child-care issues that prevent them from attending church, are you working cooperatively with the church nursery to devise a plan that meets the need? (The need to work collaboratively will be further explored later in imperative 5, "Be Complementary.") When you demonstrate to the community that you have their physical needs at heart, they will more readily accept your remedy for their spiritual malaise.

If you as finance chairperson in your church sense that certain families are having trouble managing their household income, you might consider establishing a free counseling service to provide ongoing basic information related to budgeting. I, however, believe the church should go beyond counseling. For example, some couples make financial mistakes early in their marriages, such as runaway credit card usage. Even after realizing their error and seeking counsel, they may find it very challenging to climb out of the financial quagmire they mindlessly plunged into. Perhaps a familiar adage can be applied here: "Give them a hand up, not a handout." The church could breathe life into this adage by providing a challenge grant to those couples, providing that they comply with their counselor and subsequently commit to helping others move toward financial stability.[2]

---

**Genius, in truth, means little more than the faculty of perceiving in an unhabitual way.**

*—William James*

---

As a community volunteer at the senior citizen center, are you routinely scanning the papers, pending legislation, the Internet, and other sources to be sure that trends impacting your constituency are not overlooked and opportunities missed? The crux of imperative 4, "Be discerning," is to be vigilant and watchful for indicators that will dictate the emergence of new opportunities, direction, or focus.

As a parent you also must be discerning. You cannot lead your children to excellence in school if you are not attuned to their study habits, eating patterns, social contacts, and other influences. As a parent you may never lead a civic organization or committee outside the home, but you are called to lead your children into adulthood. If you are working multiple jobs and are exhausted, observing your child's behavior and performance will be a challenge. However difficult it may be, it still does not free you from the obligation. Parents must be involved in their children's lives to determine if something is going awry. If you don't know what is normal, how can you possibly know when things have become abnormal?

Leaders at all levels, whether corporate, civic, religious, or parental, have to be able to adapt to changing conditions, much like an athletic coach. Anyone can coach when the game is progressing without incident. The real coaching occurs when conditions dictate a change in strategy. Coaches, like leaders, size up the situation and make the appropriate adjustments. Leaders have to be flexible and open to emerging events and opportunities. Unlike some who become consumed with a rigid set course, John maintained a discerning attitude and watchful eye for the one for whom he was so vigorously making preparation.

How can we discern the movement of God? We must first of all be in a continuous mode of prayer and meditation. As Nehemiah rebuilt the walls of Jerusalem with one hand on his sword, so should we as leaders work with one hand on the Word of God, testing all that we see to be sure it lines up with the Word. While this is not an exhaustive or exclusive approach, I suggest the following:

1. Pray regularly.

2. Meditate on the Word of God consistently.

3. Trust the urging of the Holy Spirit.

4. Observe your environment and note changes.

5. Never assume that God will move in a "logical" fashion (the Spirit rarely does).

Sometimes we pray for guidance and then fail to see it when it is given. If we don't like the messenger, we discount the message. If the message doesn't buttress our biases, we dismiss it as irrelevant and continue to muse without moving. If the message does not provide an answer that coincides with our intended action, we either take matters into our own hands or piously wait, granting God another opportunity to respond more to our liking. We can be like the man sitting on top of his flooded home, refusing rescue from a motorboat and a helicopter, choosing rather to "wait on the Lord." When he dies and appears before God, he asks why God permitted him to perish. God reminds the man of the motorboat and the helicopter, and points out that he refused them both!

Meditating on the Word goes beyond reading only. It requires reading followed by reflective rumination, allowing what has been read to sink in deeply and serve as the seed for inspiration and direction. The psalmist was on target when he wrote that the blessed man's "delight is in the law of the LORD; and in his law doth he meditate day and night" (Psalm 1:2).

> **What you always do before you make a decision is consult. The best public policy is made when you are listening to people who are going to be impacted.**
>
> *—Elizabeth Dole*

When Jesus was preparing to face his death, he assured his disciples that he would not leave them without a helper. He promised to send the Holy Spirit to be their companion, guide, and comforter (John 14:16, 26). Since this is the case, it is illogical for us to deny the Spirit's leaning and prompting in our lives. The Holy Spirit is here to lead us into all truth and to help us maintain our credibility as Christians. When the Spirit speaks, we are to listen and obey.

As a leader you will find that it is vitally important to be familiar with your field of endeavor so that you can recognize shifts that translate into opportunity. This is true whether you are a parent detecting changes in your child's behavior patterns or a corporate executive noticing a change in consumer spending patterns. For instance, if you were in charge of your church's transportation ministry, you would need to be attuned to the places that weekly worshipers travel from each week as an indicator of the coverage and influence of the church, and potentially the areas your ministry may have to service in the future for those without access to public or personal transportation.

As a leader, dare to be bold enough to trust God to show up in unorthodox ways. The Bible gives no indication, but I doubt that John expected Christ simply to walk down to the revival meeting with the rest of the crowd. Logic would have suggested a more dramatic entrance. But God's approach never coincides with human logic. To his credit, John the Baptist yielded to the Holy Spirit and boldly proclaimed in faith that the Messiah had arrived.

## Speaking of That . . .

God not only shows up in unorthodox ways, but he uses those most of us would overlook if we were selecting someone for a specific task. John the Baptist did not attend the local school of law, nor was he a member of the religious hierarchy. He was uneducated, rugged, hardened. God chose this peculiar man to be the forerunner of his beloved Son. Even among the disciples, Jesus chose weather-beaten fisherman, a physician, and a despised tax collector to carry out his mission. Later, needing someone to carry the gospel to the Gentiles, he commissioned Saul, a notorious persecutor of the church. As has been said, "God uses an imperfect person to preach a perfect gospel to an imperfect people." Therefore, never permit others to discredit your calling when you know for sure you have been appointed to the task. If earthly parents are smart enough to know what assignments their children are capable of handling, why should we think that the God of the universe is any less astute?

Many opportunities are lost by people failing to be alert and observant. Whether it is detecting a shift in the stock market prior to making a critical investment decision, noticing a barely perceptible weakness in an opponent during an athletic contest, or altering your planned route as the traffic pattern ahead evolves, the decision made in each of these instances has consequences, and so it is essential that each situation be considered carefully and followed by decisive action.

In the exodus account, the Israelites depart Egypt and arrive at Kadesh-barnea, the passageway to the Promised Land. After twelve spies are sent to inspect the land, the report comes back that the land is indeed bursting with bounty just as God promised. However, ten of the twelve spies are afraid of the inhabitants of Canaan and dissuade the people from possessing the land. This lack of faith in God's promise results in delayed blessing and four decades of aimless and circuitous wandering through the desert. When leaders are imperceptive and fearful of taking risks, lost opportunities are unavoidable.

Jesus, the master teacher, used a parable to describe his unexpected return. He compares his return to the arrival of a bridegroom who has ten virgins waiting for his appearance. Five of them are wise enough to bring along additional oil for their lamps in the event the bridegroom is delayed. The other five run out of oil, and while they are trying to secure more, the delayed bridegroom arrives and the five foolish virgins miss the celebration. Jesus used this parable to warn against slothfulness and unpreparedness. John the Baptist echoes this sentiment when he demonstrates by example the blessing contained in a watchful attitude while rendering service.

Although this book has been written to illustrate the role of these imperatives in church-based leadership, they are equally transferable to the private sector, and powerfully instructive.

Consider the three examples that follow of corporate organizations that experienced positive results that came from a discerning perspective followed by decisive action.

## 1. THE MINIVAN

In 1983 the chairman of the Chrysler Corporation, Lee Iacocca, introduced the Chrysler minivan as an alternative to the industry's other less commodious and fuel-efficient vehicles. It was a vehicle that he and a former subordinate at the Ford Motor Company, Hal Sperlich, had conceived while employed by Ford. Iacocca recognized that the family structure was changing and that a different kind of vehicle was necessary. Sensing that the time was right to introduce a vehicle that accommodated the needs of busy parents, especially mothers, Chrysler launched the minivan. Note that mothers were not beating down the doors at Chrysler demanding a car such as the minivan, but based upon market research and Iacocca's own savvy, the minivan emerged, sparking a revolution that continues today, as every major automaker now produces some version of a minivan. Iacocca exhibited John's imperative 4, "Be discerning."

## 2. MICROSOFT

In 1975 a very bright young computer enthusiast named Bill Gates withdrew from Harvard University to form a computer software company along with his friend and fellow student, Paul Allen. Together they built a fledgling company into today's iconic behemoth, Microsoft. When speaking of his vision for computers, Gates says, "When [we] started Microsoft 30 years ago, we had a vision of a 'computer on every desk and in every home,' which probably sounded a little too optimistic when most computers were the size of refrigerators. But we believed that personal computers would change the world. And they have."[3] Gates exhibited imperative 4, "Be discerning," in that he and Allen recognized the potential for personal computers and acted upon what they had been privileged to foresee. The key to discernment is not just in the seeing, but in the doing. Many have had hunches that went nowhere due to fear, lethargy, or indifference. When you are discerning, are you also poised to take action?

### 3. TORRID CLOTHING

A study conducted in 2006 by the Mintel market research firm indicated that 62 percent of American women wear a size 14 or larger. In fact, the plus-size clothing industry soared to $32 billion in 2005, representing a 50 percent growth from 2001.[4] Hot Topic, Inc., has a subsidiary store named Torrid that opened in 2000 to cater to this growing segment of female shoppers, providing them with stylish choices in sizes 12 to 26. They now have more than a hundred stores nationwide and also provide an online shopping option (www.torrid.com).[5] It is not hard to see how this company assessed the market trend and responded by meeting an unspoken need. They are yet another example of a company exhibiting imperative 4, "Be discerning."

## Discern and Act

John the Baptist left us with the admonition to be discerning. Which is worse: to discern and not take action or to fail to be vigilant and discerning? Both are equally blameworthy. One is a sin of commission and the other is a sin of omission. In either case, you would miss the mark. When we are afforded the advantage of a perceptive glimpse into future possibilities, it is our obligation to take action. Why? In corporate America it could be the difference between expansion and extinction. In the home it could be the difference between a marriage crumbling silently or a marriage salvaged and rescued from the statistical dunghill of divorce. In a classroom it could be the difference between a late bloomer nurtured and encouraged and a demoralized child consigned to mediocrity. In ministry it could be the difference between a life infused with hope for brighter tomorrows and one sapped of any motivation to move beyond an abject existence today.

In the next section we will examine imperative 5, "Be complementary." John will demonstrate both how to work collaboratively and how to recognize when it is time to move on. Sometimes after performing a task for so long, and so sincerely, it becomes a challenge to let go. The sports world is full of examples of coaches and athletes who refuse to accept the fact that their mission has been completed. They linger longer than they should, sometimes unwittingly bringing dishonor to themselves. Most of us have difficulty accepting change. Interim pastors, standing in the gap until a permanent pastor is called, balk when it is time to move on. Employees whose job functions are no longer required stubbornly refuse to learn new skills. A chauvinistic husband refuses to change his attitude even if it means losing his wife and family. Although change may be good, it is rarely comfortable. Yet in church, in the workplace, or at home, change is inevitable.

When you have been called to perform a task, look for the movement of God as an indication that your task has been completed, and then relinquish the reins. Imagine what a scene it would cause at Buckingham Palace if one guard would resist the changing of the guards at the prescribed time. We all have a role to play in God's divine plan. Each of our roles is predetermined with a specific beginning and end point. If we observe, at minimum, the five suggestions for discerning the movement of God (pray regularly, meditate on the Word, trust the Spirit, observe your environment, expect God to move in an illogical fashion), we are more likely to see God's hand of providential intervention. In the next imperative we explore how we are to embrace change that inevitably results from complementary collaboration.

## Points to Consider

**1.** How is discernment different than visioning?

**2.** Is discernment something that we all naturally possess? Or must it be cultivated and developed? Why?

**3.** Discuss a time when you waited on divine direction and how that direction was made known to you.

**4.** In your church ministry what unmet needs do you detect?

**5.** When has your organization missed out on a business opportunity due to failure to act decisively?

**6.** Whom do you know personally who exemplifies imperative 4, "Be discerning"?

**7.** How would your life to this point have been different if you had applied this imperative?

**8.** What changes can you make in the future to become more discerning?

# BE Complementary

Again the next day after John stood, and two
of his disciples; and looking upon Jesus as
he walked, he saith, Behold the Lamb of God!
And the two disciples heard him speak, and
they followed Jesus.

—JOHN 1:35-37

As a leader in your home, workplace, church, school, or civic organization, you soon discover that to be truly effective you must work in concert with others. Even those who fancy themselves a "Lone Ranger" are to be reminded that even his success was dependent upon Tonto. To be sure, more can be accomplished when resources and talents are pooled together in a complementary fashion to achieve an objective.

At the risk of being pedantic, I wish to differentiate between *complementary* and *complimentary*. I make the distinction between the two with an example. When former Chicago Bulls Michael Jordan and Scottie Pippen found themselves in a two-on-one fast-break situation, they often wreaked havoc on the defending opponent, finishing the break with an authoritative dunk. While returning up court, they would invariably acknowledge one another, as if to say, "Nice job." This acknowledgment was *complimentary.* The manner in which they worked together to score the basket was *complementary.* To be complementary is to be collaborative, cooperative, or conjoined rather than contradictory, competitive, or disjointed.

The source text underpinning imperative 5 informs us of the complementary nature of John the Baptist. The next day after his discerning declaration of Jesus' identity, John the Baptist was standing with two of his disciples. Jesus came toward them, and John declared once more to his disciples, "Behold the Lamb of God!" Immediately the two followed Jesus. What the Bible does not record is John's reaction to the loss of his disciples. There is no record of John complaining that Jesus was stealing his members. Nor is there record of John scolding and demanding his disciples to return to him.

---

**The leaders who work most effectively, it seems to me, never say "I." . . . They don't think "I." They think "we"; they think "team." They understand their job to be to make the team function.**

*—Peter Drucker*

---

Remember, John the Baptist, over several months at least, had influenced hundreds of repentant sinners and amassed a few disciples. He had upset the religious order, challenged conventional wisdom, and pointed to the Savior. So it would not be surprising if he were resentful of his followers leaving him and giving their allegiance to another—except that John was a man who was sure of his purpose (imperative 1), remained focused (imperative 2), and completed his assignment with humility and appreciation for the opportunity to serve (imperative 3). While the passage cited above does not record John the Baptist's reaction, we can infer his reaction by examining a complementary passage.

In John 3 we learned that Jesus and his growing band of disciples had settled in Judea and were baptizing there. Meanwhile,

John the Baptist and his followers were north of Judea along the border of Samaria and were baptizing there (vv. 22-23). John's disciples did not possess his spiritual maturity, and a few of them came to John and announced to him with some agitation— understandably, given their mindset—that the man who was with John at the Jordan was now baptizing also. Moreover, they reported, "All men come to him" (v. 26). John proceeded to remind his shaken disciples that he had already told them that he was not the Christ, "but that I am sent before him" (v. 28).

John demonstrated that he was not offended that all men were following Jesus, including two of his initial disciples; rather, he was overjoyed! "He that hath the bride is the bridegroom: but the friend of the bridegroom, which standeth and heareth him, rejoiceth greatly because of the bridegroom's voice: this my joy is therefore fulfilled. He must increase, but I must decrease" (vv. 29-30).

John is what I would characterize as a "cheerleader for change." John did not condemn his disciples' defection; he celebrated it! Effective leaders who understand their purpose and role in the broader plan will always work to quell dissension. John knew it was now time for him to move off center stage and give way to Jesus. To see the hand of God moving in your ministry can be exhilarating and affirming if you approach your charge with the right motives.

## Complementary Partnerships in Action!

Before we face the inevitability of change and varying responses to it, let's examine a few ways to form complementary partnerships—both in the church and in some effective secular examples. Then we can consider the things that keep us from being complementary in ministry and most other vocations.

In the preceding chapter, under the discussion about discerning, I acknowledged that there will be times when events will necessitate partnering with other persons or groups to meet your stated objectives. As I said, if potential passengers in your transportation ministry are reluctant to visit the church due to child-care issues, are you engaging members of the child-care ministry to develop a workable solution? Some churches are very adept at combining resources and insisting that various ministries collaborate. The leaders of those congregations recognize the interconnectedness among the ministries.

In his book *12 Steps to Congregational Transformation*, Rev. Dr. David Laubach notes the pitfall of "Lone Ranger leadership" that many pastors and even lay leaders stumble into. He describes a variety of masks that such leaders wear: Doc Do-It-Myself, Rev to the Rescue, Committee Commander, and Pastor-in-Chief. None of these Lone Rangers succeed in building the teams that a complementary leader produces. Teams, according to Laubach, "are organic and dynamic. They capitalize on individual gifts, covering one member's weakness with another's strength"—including the leader's![1]

Complementary partnership opportunities abound in ministry. Indeed, Laubach asserts that such partnerships are *the* biblical model as described by Paul in 1 Corinthians 12:12-31 and Ephesians 4:11-12 and by Peter in 1 Peter 4:10. "The leader who doesn't mentor, equip laity for the work of ministry, train interns, take the long-range view, and perform as a team player and player-coach is doomed to be a shooting star at best," Laubach warns.[2] And what is true of individual leaders is also true of ministry groups that enjoy complementary leadership.

Complementary partnership opportunities abound in ministry. In my home church the clothing ministry and the food pantry work together to meet the needs of members and nonmembers. They provide food on a recurring and/or emergency basis, along with clothing for adults and their children. The transportation ministry provides the means for getting participants to the weekly addiction ministry meeting. The media ministry, which includes still photography, provides support to the newsletter ministry. The nursery ministry sometimes provides support to parents required to participate in a mandatory forum, be it a workshop, conference, or new-member orientation. Although we have about 1,500 active members, the size of the congregation has no bearing on the need for complementary ministry. Small congregations have to pool resources due to the scarcity of available hands, and large, or mega-congregations (over two thousand attendees) must collaborate to meet the growing demands of the masses.

Warren Buffet, until recently the second richest man in the world, serves as an example from the corporate world of someone who understands the principle of complementarity. In 2006 Buffet announced his intention to transfer the majority of his wealth to the Bill and Melinda Gates Foundation. When asked why he didn't establish his own foundation, he essentially replied that Bill and Melinda are smart people and they already have a very well-run foundation, so it didn't make sense to start his own foundation when he could simply complement one that already shared his values and was operating effectively.[2] If two of the wealthiest men in the world, religious beliefs aside, can see the power in complementing rather than competing, what hinders the rest of us?

---

**A community is like a ship; everyone ought to be prepared to take the helm.**

*—Henrik Ibsen*

---

In his book *The 7 Habits of Highly Effective People,* management guru and best-selling author Stephen Covey substantiates this imperative of John the Baptist with his habit #6, "synergize." Covey's habit #6 subscribes to the principle that "the whole is greater than the sum of its parts." He is a strong proponent of collaborative decision making. As a quality management professional for twenty-six years, I have seen individuals with unique abilities and intellect achieve extraordinary results when they teamed together to optimize the contribution each made. Although trite, it is still true that "together everyone achieves more" (TEAM).

If teaming has proven to be an effective force multiplier, why do we often resist partnering with others to achieve our allegedly mutual objective? Many leaders in particular, and most people in general, are very territorial and reluctant to make any concessions that might require relinquishing hard-earned gains. It comes down to a matter of turf. In some churches the pastor is a "bishop unto himself." This authority to proceed in the manner God is specifically leading makes it very difficult to concede ground to another. (Again I refer you to Laubach's Lone Ranger chapter!) These leaders are clear in purpose and focused and perhaps are even humble and discerning. Undoubtedly, their precise vision, supported by a strategic plan, makes it more challenging and risky to collaborate with another who may have a different lens by which he or she views ministry. As we noted earlier, John the Baptist had no problems with turf. He understood the benefit of complementary ministry and how all those involved contributed to the sum total and ultimate achievement of the objective. John was not bothered in the least that Jesus was also baptizing and making disciples.

---

**We must learn our limits. We are all something, but none of us are everything.**

—*Blaise Pascal*

---

Early in his own ministry, Malcolm X vigorously opposed the nonviolent tactics employed by most in the civil rights movement, particularly Dr. Martin Luther King Jr. Yet even though he disagreed, he knew that he and King had the same ambitions for black liberation and self-sufficiency in America. In fact, Malcolm warned the dominant forces of opposition that if they did not heed King's approach, they would have to deal with his. He understood that even the two strident and diametrically opposed philosophies espoused by King and himself were ultimately complementary and assured that the concerns of black America would be heard. James H. Cone writes, "Malcolm's challenge of Martin's philosophy of nonviolence caused many whites, particularly northern liberals, to reevaluate their view of Martin moving too fast on the civil rights agenda."[4]

A second impediment to complementary ministry related to turf is the silo mentality that most churches acquire as they focus on their programs. The term *silo mentality* is drawn from the metaphor of corn and grain silos found on farms. Each one is tall and able to hold considerable quantities, and what is in one silo cannot spill over into another. Sometimes churches grow in leaps and bounds, independent and nondependent of others, rarely proactively seeking opportunities to partner. When collaboration occurs it is usually a response to a current, or coming, crisis, rather than a standard way of operating.

Those churches that collaborate with others routinely are to be commended and serve as models for others. Consider the historic impact that churches have made on such issues of social justice as the abolition of slavery, the Civil Rights Movement, and the end of apartheid in South Africa. Other congregations form powerful partnerships in response to natural disasters, such as the churches that sent volunteers and donations in the wake of the hurricanes of 2005. The possibilities for partnership extend beyond even the Christian community, as we saw when pastors, priests, rabbis, and imams gathered to intercede in prayer and public witness after the terrorist attacks of September 11, 2001. What impact would we see on this world if churches and their leaders would seek intentional partnerships to address "everyday crises" such as hunger, illiteracy, homelessness . . . the list could go on for pages!

Complementary ministry is not just "working together"; it involves assessing the mutual strengths and weaknesses of each partner and relinquishing responsibilities based on which organization is better suited for the specific task. It is about building on and optimizing collective strengths and effectively neutralizing the weaknesses that would hamper success. These complementary associations are not restricted to church collaborations. Churches should (and many do) proactively collaborate with social service agencies to provide people with needed services in a manner that is user friendly and nonthreatening or invasive. Whatever the arrangement, it is essential that scarce resources are optimized and wheels not reinvented. Recall the lesson of the Buffet and Gates collaboration.

A third reason we fail to form complementary associations is because of lack of awareness of the resources available. Many churches have therefore formed community-development corporations: A CDC is able to tap into resource providers that are legally prevented from working with religious organizations. The CDC allows service to be rendered that is informed and impacted by the values of the church. Churches not yet prepared to form a CDC should still determine who provides the services needed by their members and, at minimum, assist members with understanding the requirements for qualifying for the services.

---

**The art of leadership is saying no, not yes. It is very easy to say yes.**

—*Tony Blair*

---

Fourth, in the church some ministry leaders are reluctant to collaborate if it puts them at risk for blending into obscurity. Although they are committed to their duties, some unfortunately have suspect skills and sometimes little formal training in the disposition of their duties. They are sometimes very reluctant to partner because church is the one place they can be in charge of something. So to relinquish authority to peers, in their minds, diminishes their overall importance and value. Related to this insecurity is a dearth of people skills. A lack of these skills can result in bitter internecine conflict over issues of minutiae, needlessly scarring all affected parties. Little can be more hurtful than an inexperienced and untrained leader, no matter how committed, lashing out at another while standing behind the authority vested in his or her title. People will leave the church, either physically or emotionally, when they observe leaders engaging people in a way that is offensive. If a church is not willing to train people or to appoint leaders who already possess effective people skills, they are by default empowering ineffective leaders to seek and destroy at will.

Finally, complementary associations are sometimes not actively pursued within the church due to the pastor permitting and even fomenting a climate of competition. We see this in some Baptist churches through the "annual days" of the various ministries. Generally, each ministry works all year raising funds so that on their day they can report a larger amount of funds raised for the church than another ministry reported on their day. In some churches the congregation is divided by states of origin and each member is exhorted to maintain his or her home state's honor by assisting in various fund-raisers and activities throughout the year. Churches encourage competition because it is a proven technique for getting more congregants involved. We are all competitive to varying degrees, so to issue a rallying cry to outraise or outperform another resonates with our inborn nature. Yet there is a cost to pay when church members can only be motivated to serve when a proverbial carrot is dangled before them. The competitive teamwork that occurs when one ministry pits itself against another is effective but is short-lived and produces "champions" rather than forging a unified congregation.

Rev. E. V. Hill used to say by way of illustration that one gigantic ecclesiastical football team would accomplish the Great Commission. We are not in competition. If you can run the ball better than anyone else on the team, then the rest of us should block for you! And when the church down the street scores by taking in a convert, we all win! So it should be with all facets of ministry within the church.

## Easier Said Than Done in Business

In the business world, the downside of pitting one department against another to breed competition is that it can create adversarial relationships rather than collaborative ones. Competition should therefore be only with those from the outside. All those within are to be working toward the same goal, such that if one department succeeds, all succeed. This becomes more challenging when compensation is closely tied to performance, a practice that sends mixed signals to employees who are exhorted to work for the good of the team yet are rewarded as individuals. There are alternative ways to recognize performers while maintaining a climate that encourages and rewards all, equitably, for their collective achievement. Any good human resources director can offer plenty of ideas and examples to try.

## Your Post May Change, But Not Your Purpose

As initially suggested in imperative 1, "Be Sure," life mirrors nature, and just as we enjoy the four seasons of winter, spring, summer, and fall, so will we go through life seasons. What may have been our purpose in one life season may not be so in the next. Or said a better way, our ultimate purpose may not change, but the way we approach it may. As I said earlier, although I was formerly a choir director and singer, I now find that singing is not where my passion lies. So I take delight in singing from the pew rather than persisting in an area that is not compelling enough for me to make it my consuming priority. Even as parents we go through seasonal changes when our approach to parenting shifts. As a parent your ultimate purpose is to rear your children successfully into responsible adults. As pimply faced teenagers, your children may need more basic assurances from you—that they are pretty or handsome, that anyone would want to be their friend, that they are intelligent and capable of achieving their dreams. Later in life, after they have added skill, accomplishment, and confidence to those natural aptitudes and potential, your young adult offspring may crave affirmation of their career choice or life partner. In all seasons of parenting, it is your purpose to encourage your children to ever evolving maturity.

You may be a very effective teacher and find that the venue through which you previously exercised your natural talents has been closed off to you. This does not suggest that you are no longer called to engage your gift as an instructor; rather, it suggests that it may be time to move to another venue. See the closed door as an opportunity and not an obstruction. What you have been preordained to perform does not change. A change of post is not necessarily a change in purpose.

To be sure, aside from God's faithfulness, the only constant we can count on is change. Change is inevitable. No one can remain unchanged and unaffected by the challenges of life. We will either change for the better or for the worse—there is no middle ground. The challenge for each of us is to determine how we will respond to change.

A delightful book titled *Who Moved My Cheese?* appeared in stores a few years ago. It is a humorous and instructive tale of four mice that react in different ways to an unexpected change in their customary and established way of acquiring their daily supply of cheese. The moral of the story is that change is unavoidable, and how disruptive it is depends on our response.[5]

Change makes us uncomfortable because it forces us out of our comfort zone. Perhaps it is like holding on to that old worn sofa because over time it has adapted to the contours of our body and has become very inviting and comfortable. To replace it would mean having to take the time to break in a new sofa. So, as long as it is not gaudy and tattered, some choose to hold on and keep fluffing the cushions. You may say, "Not me—I handle change very well." Perhaps you are one of those rare people who thrives on change and spontaneity.

Let's take a quick test: Wherever you are sitting, take a moment right now and fold your arms across your chest as you normally would. Now that you are in your usual comfortable position, reverse your arms. If you naturally cross your arms by placing your left arm over your right arm, fold your right over your left. Be honest—it feels slightly awkward, doesn't it? Hold it there awhile and think about how different it feels, how strange. This simple exercise illustrates how we can unconsciously become accustomed to doing a thing a certain way, and then when asked to make the slightest adjustment, we automatically recoil.

Imagine how we respond to significant changes in our lives. Recall a time you were required to make a major change in your life and your initial reaction—not a change you initiated, but a change you were forced to make due to external circumstances. Did you rebel, or did you calmly accept it with the resignation that "All things work together for good" (Romans 8:28)?

Even when John's disciples left him to follow Jesus, he was not resentful; he rejoiced! Regrettably, sometimes pastors react like John the Baptist's disciples rather than John himself when a member announces his or her intention to unite with a different congregation. Pastors are human also, and therefore whenever a longtime member voluntarily leaves, the ego is subject to regard that action as a personal affront or repudiation. Consequently, some pastors take the change very personally and either chide the member for desiring to leave or sever ties with the member swiftly, judiciously, and immediately with a rigid and frigid finality. As difficult as it may be to do so, the pastor too must be a cheerleader for change and celebrate, not condemn.

One pastor who seems to have John's perspective is Tony Evans of the Oak Cliff Bible Fellowship (OCBF) in Dallas. His website gives an indication of his general spirit and attitude about members changing churches. Under "Church History" Evans provides a chronology of the OCBF. While many churches maintain a running account of the church's evolution, few celebrate the contributions of past staff members like the

OCBF. I list below some of the entries in one of the four epochal periods by which they divide their church history, acknowledging the contributions of leaders previous and present:

## 1988–1993

- Dr. "Sonny" Acho, a licensed psychologist and native of Nigeria, joined the staff as Associate Pastor of Fellowship.

- Clarence Diggs, Minister of Music, went home to be with the Lord.

- Rev. Warren Mattox resigned as Associate Pastor of Outreach to accept a position at Moody Bible Institute in Chicago.

- Rev. Larry Mercer resigned as Associate Pastor of Christian Education to become superintendent of the Dallas County Youth Village, a facility for troubled and at-risk youth.

- Rev. Roger Skepple, a Dallas Seminary graduate, was hired as Associate Pastor of Christian Education.

- Rev. Sylvester London was appointed Interim Associate Pastor of Worship, having served in the music ministry for many years.[6]

Notice how the history of OCBF celebrates and commemorates the contributions of its leaders, including the deceased minister of music and those who resigned from the OCBF to pursue other vocational callings. I cannot read into the mind and heart of Dr. Evans, but because of what is preserved in the official church record, I can safely conclude that he fully supported the decisions of Mattox and Mercer. Evans perpetually celebrates their contribution and their decision through the church history posted on the website for viewing by all. This is the complementary attitude that John the Baptist modeled and what I believe will contribute to our effectiveness as leaders.

In the first five imperatives, we examined essential attributes for effective leadership. In the next imperative, "Be Uncompromising," we will be challenged to consider our values and stand for our principles and beliefs even at the risk of personal peril. For many this imperative will be the most difficult to embrace because it requires a willingness to lay everything on the line for what we believe.

## Points to Consider

**1.** When is being competitive more appropriate than being complementary?

**2.** How do you generally react to unanticipated change?

**3.** Discuss the notion that a change in post is not necessarily a change in purpose.

**4.** Why do you think some people struggle with complementary partnerships?

**5.** Does your church or organization have ways of showing how it values the contributions of former and current leaders? What are they?

**6.** Whom do you personally know who exemplifies imperative 5, "Be complementary"?

**7.** How would your life to this point have been different if you had applied this imperative? How can you apply it now?

# BEUncompromising

Herod had laid hold on John, and bound him,
and put him in prison for Herodias' sake, his
brother Philip's wife. For John said unto him,
It is not lawful for thee to have her.

—MATTHEW 14:3-4

Imperative 1, "Be sure," is the most critical of all seven imperatives, because without purpose we would have no impetus to achieve. The most difficult imperative to embrace and live out, however, is imperative 6, "Be uncompromising."

I am not speaking of the compromise between two or more parties to reach an amicable settlement. That type of compromise is essential for progress. I have been married twenty-two years, and I can attest that without compromise by both partners, the road to happiness will be rocky. As the colloquial adage goes, "If Mama ain't happy, ain't nobody happy." Compromise is not limited to spouses. I grew up in an era when most households had only one television around which everyone gathered. I recall the many times my sister and I negotiated an agreement over which program we would watch on a particular night. I am a diehard Western fan and she was heavily into

*Beach Blanket Bingo, Tammy,* and *Viva Las Vegas* (the Elvis version). So we learned to compromise early in life, and as a result I gained an unexpected appreciation for Annette Funicello and she for John Wayne.

But in this imperative John the Baptist instructs us to be uncompromising. At first blush this advise appears contradictory to the admonishment in the preceding chapter to be complementary. How can we be both complementary and uncompromising at the same time? How do we encourage collaboration and teamwork on one hand and insist on the other hand that everyone be uncompromising? The answer to these questions is contextual, and if we examine John's predicament as recorded in the scriptural reference underlying this chapter, I believe the distinction between the two will become understandable.

**Don't compromise yourself. You are all you've got.**

*—Janis Joplin*

Recall that in imperative 2, "Be focused," John the Baptist was singularly focused on calling men and women to repentance in preparation for the Messiah spoken of by the prophets. He preached with urgency and without equivocation. As the prophetic voice of his day, he knew the import of his assignment and did not mince words; precious lives and souls were at stake. John did not give a free pass to anyone when it came to issues of morality and justice. Despite imperative 3, "Be humble," although he was unassuming and not intoxicated by the public adulation, John was no coward, including when it came to withstanding the pious and pompous priesthood. He called them a generation of vipers. John essentially became the moral conscience of his day, sparing no one. Not even Herod.

Herod Antipas, ruler of the regions of Galilee (sixty miles north of Jerusalem) and Perea (thirty miles east of Jerusalem) was married to the daughter of an Arabian king, but after becoming enamored with his half brother's wife, Herodias, he decided to marry her. So Herod Antipas divorced his wife, and Herodias deserted her husband, Philip. Add to this the incestuous fact that Herodias was a distant niece as well as an in-law, and Herod Antipas was in violation of the law. John was morally compelled to speak out against their wrongful marriage, and his temerity resulted in imprisonment and ultimately execution.

Imperative 6, "Be uncompromising," is the most difficult of all the imperatives because it requires a leader to disregard personal peril. John spoke out against the ruling authority during an era when it was dangerous to speak against the status quo. In America we have a Constitution that permits us to rail against all three branches of government, and even encourages such debate. During John's day no such latitude existed. One had to have an unusual depth of character to speak against an act that others merely winked at. John's command to be uncompromising speaks to our integrity and the extent to which we are unwilling to hedge and overlook behavior that clashes with our principles.

John the Baptist's imperative 6 reveals that effective leadership is risky because it requires an immovable stance on issues of integrity, morality, and justice. Does this mean that leaders are infallible and sinless? Absolutely not! Leaders struggle the same as followers, plus a leader is always under the microscope of public opinion. A leader bears the burden of urging others to a high standard while knowing all too well the chinks in his or her own armor. However, to the average person, leaders advocating righteousness while displaying defects are viewed as hypocritical and insincere. In reality the majority of effective leaders are passionate and well intentioned, often placing their mission above spouses, children, families, and friends.

John the Baptist was no different. Even though Jesus said there was no other like John, John was not exempt from the Pauline declaration that all have sinned and come short of the glory of God (Romans 3:23). Like all of us, John undoubtedly had his own challenges, of which there is no record. We do know, however, that haughtiness and conceit were not among them. This selfless emissary, however flawed in other areas of his life, was singularly focused on seeing sinners purified in preparation for the coming Messiah. It may surprise some that those who are called to take a stand in the most public and visible forums feel the least adequate due to their own personal peccadilloes. They, like John the Baptist, stand upright to decry unjust and immoral behavior with a clarion voice while hunched over under the burden of some unmentionable indiscretion.

What was the source of John's boldness? Certainly the Spirit of God emboldened him, but what else may have fortified his faith and caused him to rely on the Spirit to sustain him when he would have to stand alone? I believe he was helped by his history. As the son of a priest and a mother descended from no less than the priest Aaron, John most likely had been adequately made aware of the Law and the Prophets. In those books he would have learned about the boldness of those who preceded him, such as Shadrach, Meshach, Abednego, and Daniel. Recall that these Hebrews were captured by the Babylonians and given a place of honor because of their superior skill, ability, and intellect. But a time came when the king decreed that all would have to kneel and worship a golden idol at the sound of the flute, harp, and other musical instruments. When the Hebrews refused, they were brought before the king for judgment. The king reminded them that all who refused to bow were to be cast into a fiery furnace. The Hebrews responded, "O Nebuchadnezzar . . . if it be so, our God whom we serve is able to deliver us from the burning fiery furnace, and he will deliver us out of thine hand, O king. But if not, be it known unto thee, O king, that we will not serve thy gods, nor worship the golden image which thou has set up" (Daniel 3:16-18).

As John the Baptist commands us with imperative 6, we must be uncompromising when it comes to issues of principle and morality, even if our stance is unpopular and potentially life threatening. These Hebrews knew of the one true God and his commandment that no other god be placed before him. Aligned on the side of rightness, they courageously resolved to trust God for their safekeeping.

John also drew from the example of Daniel, who was cast into a den of lions for refusing to obey King Darius's prohibition against praying for thirty days to any man or god besides the king. The record says that even though Daniel knew the king's decree had been signed and implemented, he continued his ritual of facing Jerusalem, his native homeland, three times daily as he prayed. The king subsequently and remorsefully had Daniel cast into the den of lions with a final exhortation: "Thy God whom thou servest continually, he will deliver thee" (Daniel 6:16). In each of these instances, the Hebrews chose death over denial, annihilation over assimilation, afterlife over appeasement, execution over excuses.

It is the responsibility of intellectuals to speak the truth and expose lies.

—*Noam Chomsky*

We can also see that this imperative to be uncompromising was manifest in the lives of the first-century church leaders, particularly Peter. Admittedly, during Jesus' final days on earth, Peter faltered and denied any allegiance to him. Nevertheless, after rising from the dead, Jesus reaffirmed Peter and restored his confidence—so much so, we are told, that when confronted by the religious hierarchy and reprimanded for preaching the gospel, Peter and other disciples declared, "We ought to obey God rather than men" (Acts 5:29). After much debate the council beat Peter and the apostles and commanded them to stop speaking in the name of Jesus. Here again we see that these early church leaders placed principle over personal peril. John the Baptist commands us to do likewise; he urges us to be uncompromising.

Lay leaders in the church are not exempt from John's command to be principled leaders who do not compromise. In the Baptist church one of the most popular ministries is the choir. Even those with a modicum of vocal ability are generally welcome. Invariably, every choir establishes rules of conduct for its members to ensure consistency in behavior and deportment. Far too often, however, the rules are not universally enforced. The star tenor and lead might miss the most recent rehearsal and even arrive after the choir is in place, but the director overlooks these infractions because the tenor is slated to sing two solos that Sunday. This double standard is never lost on the rest of the choir and usually leads to dissension and resentment of the director. A leader who embraces imperative 6 will not compromise, but will hold every choir member to the same standard, regardless of the impact on the choir's overall sound and delivery. Maintaining the respect of the group far outweighs currying the favor of any one individual. When the leader condones violations of the agreed-upon rules, the following results:

- Resentment of the leader and the one given preferential treatment

- Increasing disregard by others for the rules of conduct

- Loss of respect for the leader's authority

- Destructive gossiping and murmuring

Conversely, when the leader enforces the rules, he or she can expect:

- Respect of all group members

- Commitment to excellence and precision

- Focused members

- Increased participation and interest in membership

When a leader chooses to enforce the rules, he or she may have to endure some unpleasantness. Be assured that a few members will unjustly form an opinion of the leader that is hurtful:

- Who died and left him in charge?

- She thinks she's "all that."

- He puts his pants on the same as I do.

- She is an unfeeling and uncaring dictator.

Despite these unjustified accusations, an effective leader has to stand on principle and endure any slurs that might follow. An effective leader does the appropriate thing regardless of pressure to compromise. If you are the type of person who has a need to be well liked, imperative 6 will be difficult for you to embrace.

We all have heard the saying "It's lonely at the top." This is largely because good leaders remain true to their convictions even when detractors line up to point out the folly in their beliefs. Whether you are a leader of a major corporation or the leader of the local neighborhood-watch group, you may find it challenging to stand for what you know to be right when the vocal minority storms your door. (Paradoxically, your supporters, the majority, are silent.) If you are risk-averse, you will find leadership to be a very unnerving experience. Good leaders have an end goal and are compelled to see it to fruition, even at the risk of personal peril or abandonment. John the Baptist paid the ultimate penalty for his beliefs. Some have suggested that John is not much of an example of leadership given that it cost him his life. In imperative 7, I offer a counterperspective demonstrating, not the lunacy of his death, but the efficacy of it.

There comes a time in the life of every leader when his or her commitment will be tested. Are you as a leader able to stay the course when the waves of dissent are crashing over your bow?

What will you do when those closest to you are split on the rightness of your decision? How will you react to those who will attempt to silence you with either a threat or a treat? What do you do when even your mother disagrees? Such are the decisions a leader faces.

I will never forget my first encounter with imperative 6. It occurred when I was in high school. I was captain of the varsity basketball team, not because I was the best player, but because of my levelheaded approach. Being captain was fun and not demanding. My primary function was to join the referees and opposing players at midcourt to review the rules before each game. I also seemed to enjoy a bit more latitude with the officials when expressing dismay over a questionable call. Serving as captain of the team was a great honor with few risks—or so I thought.

---

**A leader takes people where they want to go. A great leader takes people where they don't necessarily want to go, but ought to be.**

*—Rosalynn Carter*

---

One day two of our better players violated the team rules. Our coaches were visibly disturbed and decided to permit the team to determine the degree of punishment the two violators deserved. To my horror the coaches gave me the responsibility to convene the team meeting and emerge with our decision. The moment the door closed behind the exiting coaches, the bargaining and rationalizing began, all directed at me! You may recall under imperative 3, "Be humble," the discussion about formal and informal leaders. Well, one of the violators was the informal leader of the team, and consequently the majority opinion in the locker room was to be as lenient as possible without appearing soft.

Admittedly, the infraction warranted at least a two-game sus-pension, but after the unrelenting arm twisting, I assented to take our verdict to the coaches. When I informed the coaches of our decision, the crestfallen looks on their faces spoke volumes to me. Without uttering a word their faces said, "After all we've tried to instill in you young men about responsibility, teamwork, and honor, you return with this weak punishment for the two teammates who essentially let you down?" Since they had agreed previously to accept our decision, they upheld it, but I will never forget the look of disappointment on their faces as I mumbled our decision. I will carry that look to my grave, but it was so powerful that I promised myself that no one else would ever again have to give me such a look for failing to stand for what I knew to be just and right.

To further illustrate imperative 6, "Be uncompromising," I draw upon the life of Muhammad Ali, the self-proclaimed "greatest of all time" boxer and a humanitarian. In 1964 Ali, then using his birth name, Cassius Clay, upset the formidable Sonny Liston to become the youngest heavyweight champion in boxing history at that time. He was brash, outspoken, and charismatic; people either loved him or loathed him. In spite of dissenters his future was bright. Some might say that "he had the world in a jar, and the stopper in his hand." But in 1967 he refused induction into the U.S. Army based on his religious beliefs and was subsequently banned from boxing for three years. He was also sentenced to five years in prison (which he did not serve, as his case was being appealed). History vindi-cated him in the end, but in the meantime, Ali was willing to stand on his principles even if it cost his means of livelihood and the trappings of fame. An effective leader accepts the inevitabil-ity of personal pain and seldom permits this specter to dissuade him from a moral and just course of action.

Another example of uncompromising leadership can be seen in the life of William Wilberforce, a British parliament member and impassioned abolitionist. With the backing of some key friends, he became the relentless voice for the abolition of both the slave trade in England and the institution of slavery in total. It was a task that took nearly forty years to complete. Despite the unpopularity of his position, he continued to introduce legislation each year calling for the abolishment, first of the slave trade and later of slavery. Aside from being a moral issue, it was an economic issue. At the time he began his crusade, nearly every businessman in England was profiting in some way from the trade of African slaves.[1] Thus, we can imagine the animosity others felt toward him for his unprecedented stance. He was ridiculed by some and accused of hypocrisy for not championing with equal fervor the cause of Britain's indigenous poor. Yet Wilberforce undauntedly persisted until the British slave trade was abolished in 1807. It would take another twenty-six years before slavery was officially abolished in all of Britain and its territories and colonies in 1833.

> [Reformers] who are really in earnest must be willing to be anything or nothing in the world's estimation, and publicly and privately, in season and out, avow their sympathy with despised and persecuted ideas and their advocates, and bear the consequences.
>
> —*Susan B. Anthony*

On the American political scene we find another example of uncompromising leadership in the person of Ronald Reagan, one of the most popular and polarizing presidents of the twentieth century. During President Reagan's two terms, the threat of global nuclear war was undeniable. Reagan's arms race is credited with dismantling the Soviet economy and, unpredictably, dissolving the Soviet Union. He was characterized as a Hollywood cowboy who viewed things in black and white. Some of the stances he took were unpopular, but he never publicly succumbed to the criticism. One example of his resolve involved a standoff with the federal Professional Air Traffic Controllers Organization. Federal employees were not legally permitted to strike. Reagan, a former president of the Screen Actors Guild and union sympathizer, saw the issue simply as twelve thousand federal controllers violating the law and creating havoc and public safety challenges. He warned the controllers that if they chose to strike, he would execute his duty and permanently dismiss them from service. As a recently elected president, this was not a popular stance to take, but his personal sense of law and order dictated that the federal employees honor their obligation. As the highest ranking federal executive, he was compelled to take a stand regardless of the political fallout and enforce the law.

Contrary to what some might think, the wealthiest among us are not reproachfully self-absorbed, but when required, are more than willing to take a stand for their beliefs, no matter how unpopular or politically sensitive. The *New York Times* published a story on February 14, 2001, that began, "Some 120 wealthy Americans, including Warren E. Buffet, George Soros and the father of William H. Gates, are urging Congress not to repeal taxes on estates and gifts."[2] President Bush desired to repeal the inheritance tax, which affected estates exceeding $3 million. These 120 who had the most to gain by this repeal vociferously opposed it, declaring it "bad for our democracy, our economy and our society." Mr. Buffet opined that it would be unwise for massive quantities of wealth to pass from generation to generation untaxed. Left unchecked this wealth would compound and potentially be used to influence every aspect of society, some positively, some negatively. While these wealthy persons' stance did not put their lives at risk, it certainly established them as a target for all those who oppose taxation of the wealthy. They understand the purpose of wealth, and consequently it went against their moral compass to sit by quietly while the president attempted to appease a few to the probable detriment of many. Gates, Buffet, and the others are tangible examples of John's imperative to be uncompromising.

The Bible does not record the exact words, but the immediate imprisonment of John the Baptist for his indicting comments makes it evident that he was being told to mind his own business. Similarly, when Dr. Martin Luther King dared to question the necessity of war, he was told to stick to issues of domestic civil rights. Leaders who are guided by the authority of God's Word are often required to move into the comfort zone of others. Naturally this foray is considered an invasion and is met with vehement and often cruel resistance. As a leader you may have to confront, in love, your followers about an area of their lives that hinders effectiveness. You can anticipate resistance and possibly a direct "It's none of your business." A leader who is concerned about the whole person will not be deterred, but will speak the truth firmly and with a tone that is lined with seriousness yet draped in compassion. This is the most difficult of all the imperatives to live out, because, like the gospel of Christ, it has a built-in offense. When such a confrontation is required be sure to do the following:

1. Pray for clarity of speech and receptivity from the individual(s).

2. Verbally acknowledge their strengths and contributions.

3. Provide context for your concern and the impact of their behavior.

4. Listen, listen, listen.

5. State expectations and seek commitment to a change in behavior.

6. Always focus on the individual's behavior and not the individual.

Recognize that sometimes your message will not be received no matter how you deliver it. Moreover, sometimes the message requires a more strident delivery commensurate to the severity of the behavior. If an individual is not amenable to altering his or her behavior, then more drastic steps may be required. I am reminded of a former local electronics manufacturing company in Central Pennsylvania that, when implementing a new concept, used to say, "When we can't change management—we *change* management!"

When leaders adhere to the "Be uncompromising" imperative, they establish a standard of integrity. When applied, it helps guard against such things as the corporate financial scandals that have received national attention. When leaders stand up for "unpopular" principles, they set a tone and create a climate of civility and honor that endures well beyond their lifetimes. John the Baptist and many other heroes recognized this, and we are indebted to them for their willingness to draw a line in the sand for integrity and justice.

The final imperative makes all of the sacrifice, scorn, challenges, trials, and criticisms that come with leadership bearable. In imperative 7, "Be encouraged," we find insight on how to stay the course despite seemingly impossible odds or marginal progress.

## Points to Consider

**1.** How does being complementary support and not contradict being uncompromising?

**2.** When should a law be challenged for being unjust?

**3.** Why do you suppose some leaders struggle with this imperative?

**4.** What are the negative consequences that follow a leader who is not uncompromising?

**5.** Describe a time when you were tested as a leader and compelled to choose principles over personal peril?

**6.** Whom do you personally know who exemplifies imperative 6, "Be uncompromising"?

**7.** How would your life to this point have been different if you had applied this imperative? How can you apply it now?

# BE Encouraged

> Go and shew John again those things which ye do hear and see: The blind receive their sight, and the lame walk, the lepers are cleansed, and the deaf hear, the dead are raised up, and the poor have the gospel preached to them.
>
> —MATTHEW 11:4-5

We have already seen in the first six imperatives that John the Baptist was a leader worthy of emulation. Although a man of modest means, he used his God-given abilities to make an impact on those around him. Like John, each of us can use these same character traits to our advantage and make a noteworthy contribution at whatever level of leadership we are placed.

John commands us to *be sure* of our calling and purpose. If your purpose is not blatantly clear, then undertake the task of discovering your raison d'être. Aside from developing a personal relationship with God, discovering your life purpose should be your most compelling preoccupation. Once identified, it will transform your thinking and replace casual existence with consuming passion!

John compels us to *be focused* and steadfast in our calling, regardless of how others may unwittingly entice us to swerve from our duty. A good understanding of our mission will limit the tendency to overextend and delve into counterproductive activities. When we are laser-focused on our purpose, we not only achieve our intended result, but we model effective stewardship for others to mimic.

John charges us to *be humble* as we carry out the tasks assigned to us. Despite how favorably others may respond to us or how laudatory their comments may be, John directs us to approach our tasks with true humility. To be genuine is to lead because of an inescapable destiny rather than unchecked ambition. Genuine leaders view leadership as a privilege to serve rather than a permit to subjugate.

---

**Leadership can be thought of as a capacity to define oneself to others in a way that clarifies and expands a vision of the future.** *—Edwin H. Friedman*

---

John constrains us to *be discerning* and watchful for indicators that God is doing something new and fresh, for indicators that a change of strategy or a changing of the guard is required. Leaders cast in the mold of John are vigilant and watchful for conditions impacting their mission. An inattentive leader may miss a critical and unrecoverable opportunity.

John challenges us to *be complementary* as we lead others, realizing that we rarely achieve anything of lasting significance wholly independent of others. An effective leader understands the value of collaboration and is not threatened by others who are working toward the same aim, even if by different methods. That leader will also celebrate change as an inevitable occurrence and not a litmus test for another's loyalty.

John calls us to righteous confrontation by insisting that we *be uncompromising* in regard to ethics, morality, fairness, and justice. An effective leader must resolve to choose principles over personal peril. Most will struggle with this imperative because the stakes can be detrimental to our career, public perception, popularity, and/or personal safety. To emulate John is to be willing to stand alone if necessary in our decision making and to strive for an ethical standard that exceeds that of the minimalist.

In this final imperative, John entreats us to *be encouraged*. The source text at the beginning of this chapter is a direct response to an inquiry made to Jesus by John's disciples. John had been imprisoned for his fearless indictment of Herod's immoral behavior, as covered in the preceding chapter.

While in prison awaiting an uncertain fate, John sent word to Jesus asking if Jesus was indeed the Messiah, the long-awaited Savior. Having discerned Jesus' identity at the Jordan, he surely must have felt that before long, and certainly in his lifetime, Jesus would establish his kingdom. That Jesus permitted him to remain imprisoned caused John even more confusion and puzzlement. So John sent for a word of confirmation. I don't believe John was only anxious about the prospect of death; rather, he did not wish to perish without an affirming word from Jesus that his life's work was indeed fruitful and that his hope was not in vain. Jesus' response detailing the unprecedented miracles allayed John's concerns and brought closure to an effective ministry. Not long afterward, Herod had John the Baptist beheaded.

Incidentally, according to Jewish historian Flavius Josephus, the Jews believed that this unwarranted and impulsive execution of John led to an attack by King Aretas of Arabia who routed Herod's army. The Jews regarded the defeat as punishment from God for executing John, "a good man [who] commanded the Jews to exercise virtue, both as to righteousness towards one another, and piety towards God, and so to come to baptism."[1]

There are those who would question the merits of lifting John the Baptist as an exemplar of leadership when his own life ended prematurely by decapitation. To see him only as a man who was beheaded for his beliefs is to miss the subtlety. John demonstrates that a selfless leader pursues his or her chosen course with no illusion that experiencing success is guaranteed. An effective leader from John's ilk knows that the mission is paramount and that where one leader leaves off, another takes up. Of course, sometimes an effective leader lives to see the fulfillment of his or her mission. Three examples are worth reviewing.

President Abraham Lincoln presided over the most tumultuous period in America's history. His primary goal was to quell the rebellion and bring the seceding states back into the Union. For four agonizing years, the country was engaged in a conflict that pitted family against family, depending on their ideological stance on slavery. The cost to preserve the Union was incalculable when measured by loss of life and property. Yet Lincoln determined that the savagery of slavery warranted the sacrifice. He endured countless sleepless nights and emotional fits, but he never wavered on his objective to see the Union preserved. Finally, on April 9, 1865, General Robert E. Lee surrendered the Confederate Army to General Ulysses S. Grant at the Appomattox Courthouse. Relieved and weary, Lincoln attended Ford's Theatre on Good Friday, April 14, and was shot by actor John Wilkes Booth, a confederate sympathizer. On April 15, 1865, exactly six days after seeing his goal realized, Lincoln died.

> You gain strength, courage, and confidence by every experience in which you really stop to look fear in the face. You must do the thing which you think you cannot do.
>
> —*Eleanor Roosevelt*

In India, Mohandas K. Gandhi devoted the latter half of his life to the liberation of India from British rule. He never held any political office, yet he was revered and respected for his moral stance and humility. An indication of India's respect for Gandhi was the title of honor bestowed upon him, *mahatma*. When the possibility of independence grew brighter, dissension arose among the Hindu and Muslim factions as each wanted independence from Britain and from each other. Despite his reservations, Gandhi assented to the division of India into the majority Hindu country of India and the Muslim country of Pakistan. The British parliament granted independence to Pakistan on August 14, 1947, and to India on August 15, 1947. There was bitter enmity between the two factions. On January 30, 1948, a Hindu, still angry at Gandhi's concession, assassinated him at gunpoint. Within five months of seeing his beloved India free of British rule, Gandhi was dead at age seventy-eight.

Antoinette Brown Blackwell was the first woman ordained as a minister in the United States—and she used her religious faith in service to the broader agenda of women's suffrage. She began speaking in church when still a child and pursued her education at Oberlin College (1847), which barred her as a female from public speaking and rhetoric courses, and Oberlin Seminary (1850), which refused her a degree or ordination, also because of her gender. That same year, she participated in the Women's Rights Convention in Worcester, Massachusetts. In 1853 the Congregational Church ordained her as the first regular Protestant minister in the country. Illness and theological differences later led her to separate from that denomination, but she simply turned her attention to focus on women's rights. Unlike many of her contemporaries, Blackwell wanted to improve women's status in society at large, not merely obtain their right to vote. Her feeling was that religion could aid that cause—and that the vote would only transform women's condition if it led to opportunities for women in leadership. In 1878, Oberlin College finally awarded Blackwell an honorary master's degree, followed by an honorary doctorate in 1908. And in 1920, Blackwell was the sole participant in the 1850 Women's Rights Convention alive to see the Nineteenth Amendment signed into law. In the 1920 election, at age 95, she cast her vote for Warren G. Harding. She died the following year.[2]

These three great leaders of history achieved their missions but died shortly thereafter (violent deaths in the cases of Lincoln and Gandhi). John the Baptist was not so fortunate to see his mission come to fruition. He died not having literally seen the fulfillment of Jesus' ascension to power, but he received enough assurance from Jesus' reply to his inquiry to know that his efforts were fruitful. There are others in American history who, like John, were individuals of purpose and never saw the full achievement of their goal.

President John F. Kennedy captured the imagination, hope, and aspiration of a nation. He came into office at a time when the Soviet Union was a real threat to democracy and world peace. During a midyear State of the Union presentation to Congress on May 25, 1961, President Kennedy made a case for not falling further behind the Russians in space exploration. He was so bold as to say, "I believe that this nation should commit itself to achieving the goal, before this decade is out, of landing a man on the moon and returning him safely to the earth."[3] With this clearly stated national mission, the course was established. On July 20, 1969, a mere five months before the end of the decade, the mission was fulfilled when Neil Armstrong became the first man to set foot on the moon. Unfortunately, President Kennedy never lived to see his stated mission completed. On November 22, 1963, he was assassinated in Dallas.

Who can forget the stirring prophetic declaration of Dr. Martin Luther King Jr. on the eve of his assassination, as he exhorted black Americans to persevere and trust God for deliverance? It was there, in response to a plea for assistance from the striking black garbage workers of Memphis, that he declared:

> Well, I don't know what will happen now. We've got some difficult days ahead. But it doesn't matter with me now. Because I've been to the mountaintop. And I don't mind. Like anybody, I would like to live a long life. Longevity has its place. But I'm not concerned about that now. I just want to do God's will. And He's allowed me to go up to the mountain. And I've looked over. And I've seen the promised land. I may not get there with you. But I want you to know tonight, that we, as a people will

get to the promised land. And I'm happy, tonight. I'm not worried about anything. I'm not fearing any man. Mine eyes have seen the glory of the coming of the Lord.[4]

The next day, April 4, 1968, King was assassinated on the balcony of the Lorraine Motel. One could argue that the fulfillment of King's dream is not yet complete, although considerable progress has been made, but my point is, like Kennedy, King had a purpose and vision for America and did not live to see its fulfillment.

> Do not be daunted by the enormity of the world's grief. Do justly, now. Love mercy, now. Walk humbly, now. You are not obligated to complete the work, but neither are you free to abandon it.
>
> *—Attributed to the Talmud*

When the causes you are championing are just and right, your perspective changes. You no longer focus on yourself but on the attainment of the goal. The acclaim of others becomes irrelevant. I'm reminded of a gospel song with the refrain:

I don't have to be the one to tell the story;
I don't have to be the one to get the glory;
Not in title or status, all that I ask
Is that you use me.
I stand humbly before thee.
Lord, use me.

When you are focused and understand your role in God's ultimate plan, you can endure many things, even to the point of sacrificing your life. As Dr. King stated, "Longevity has its place," but when we are driven by a higher purpose, nothing else matters. Your sole aim is to bring God glory through your faithful obedience to the task assigned to you.

### Can I Get a Witness?

While I am sure that I am on solid footing, it never hurts to summon someone to the stand to substantiate your claim. I recall the story of Joseph, the young dreamer who was sold into slavery by his jealous older brothers. Joseph was falsely accused, jailed, and abandoned before God elevated him to his chosen position of service. As a result of Joseph's commitment and steadfastness, God permitted Joseph to die peacefully at an old age. However, before his death he required an oath of the children of Israel, saying, "God will surely visit you, and bring you out of this land . . . And ye shall carry up my bones from hence" (Genesis 50:24-25). Joseph was speaking in faith because he knew that the land of promise was in Canaan and that God would most certainly permit his people to return home. Effective leaders do not place time restrictions on God to act, but they know God will act.

Consider Moses. After Joseph died, a new pharaoh ascended to the throne of Egypt, and he dealt harshly with the Hebrew slaves. God specifically chose Moses for the task of delivering them from Egypt to Canaan. He had hoped to lead them into the fertile land personally, but because of an earlier act of disobedience, God only permitted him to view the Promised Land from Mount Pisgah. The Bible does not record Moses' reaction, and I believe it is because, like all leaders certain of purpose, he was more concerned with the Hebrews making it safely to Canaan than he was with his own welfare.

The apostle Paul left Christ's followers with encouraging words about the Lord's return:

> But I would not have you to be ignorant, brethren, concerning them which are asleep, that ye sorrow not, even as others which have no hope. . . . For this we say unto you by the word of the Lord, that we which are alive and remain unto the coming of the Lord shall not prevent them which are asleep. For the Lord himself shall descend from heaven with a shout, with the voice of the

archangel, and with the trump of God: and the dead in Christ shall rise first: Then we which are alive and remain shall be caught up together with them in the clouds, to meet the Lord in the air: and so shall we ever be with the Lord. (1 Thessalonians 4:13, 15-17)

This passage is evidence that Paul and other saints in his day fully expected Jesus to return within their lifetime. Paul spent his entire ministry compelling others to accept Jesus as Lord and to expect his imminent return. He suffered persecution of every stripe for his belief.

---

**If your actions inspire others to dream more, learn more, do more and become more, you are a leader.**

*—John Quincy Adams*

---

Yet as Paul neared his end at the hand of Emperor Nero, he penned his second letter to his protégé Timothy, admonishing him to stand in the face of adversity and opposition. After many such words of instruction and exhortation, he concluded with, "I have fought a good fight, I have finished my course, I have kept the faith: henceforth there is laid up for me a crown of righteousness, which the Lord, the righteous judge, shall give me at that day: and not to me only, but unto all them also that love his appearing" (2 Timothy 4:6-8). Now that he is about to die, Paul essentially says to Timothy, "My living has not been in vain. I lived out my purpose, and even if I don't get to see the Lord return, I will now go to him and receive my reward. I am not daunted; I am not discouraged; I have been faithful, and my soul is encouraged!"

As we endeavor to do the work to which we are divinely appointed, we can become discouraged. When choir members won't consistently come to rehearsal, it's tempting to say, "I quit." When substance abusers continually relapse, it is difficult not to give up and ask, "Why do I bother?" When congregations resist the direction that God is trying to take them, the human tendency is to say, "Fine—I'm out of here!" When your children repeatedly drag you through the revolving doors of the courthouse due to their disobedient lifestyle, you just "wanna holla"! When you are at your lowest point of despair and frustration, God has a knack for changing events so you can see that your efforts are not fruitless but are worth it all. Martin Luther King experienced it when he caught a glimpse of racial equality; Moses experienced it when he peeked over into the Promised Land; and John experienced it when he heard the report that Jesus was who he said he was. Our challenge is to be as determined to trust God and take comfort in the small victories that assure us of eventual success. Though it may seem dark, the dawn is fast approaching. Hold on and be encouraged, "forasmuch as ye know that your labour is not in vain" (1 Corinthians 15:58). Now go forth and lead like a wild man!

## Points to Consider

**1.** How can a person be motivated to achieve even though the end results are uncertain?

**2.** Why is it necessary for a leader to be encouraged?

**3.** Is it better for the leader to be encouraged by others or to find ways to self-encourage?

**4.** What are the consequences of a leader who is not encouraged?

**5.** How do you encourage yourself as a leader in times of adversity?

**6.** Whom do you personally know who exemplifies imperative 7, "Be encouraged"?

**7.** How would your life to this point have been different if you had applied this imperative? How can you apply it now?

# NOTES

## Imperative 1: Be Sure

1. This African American folk song has varying lyrics and multiple verses. The version cited contains the words I recall from my childhood.

2. Langston Hughes, "Harlem" (1951).

3. John Eldredge, *Wild at Heart* (Nashville: Nelson, 2001), 5, 57.

4. Coretta Scott King, *My Life with Martin Luther King, Jr.* (New York: Penguin/Puffin Books, 1994), 42.

## Imperative 2: Be Focused

1. Untitled hymn, Thomas Rawson Taylor, 1835, in *The Baptist Hymnal* (Valley Forge, Pa.: Judson, 1920), hymn 677, p. 211.

2. Roland Martin live event special, "What Would Jesus Really Do?" CNN.com transcript, 2007, 1–11.

3. "Our Mission Statement," benjerry.com (accessed October 25, 2007).

4. "Company Overview," google.com (accessed October 25, 2007).

5. Kate O'Sullivan, "Kremed!" *CFO Magazine*, June 1, 2005, 1–6 (accessed at CFO.com).

6. Ibid.

## Imperative 3: Be Humble

1. James H. Cone, *Martin & Malcolm & America: A Dream or a Nightmare?* (Maryknoll, NY: Orbis, 1993), 300.

2. During the vacant pulpit of the Greater Zion Missionary Baptist Church, 1987–89, Rev. Cleophus J. LaRue Jr. was invited to preach. His sermon topic was "How to Make a Name for Yourself" (Harrisburg, Pa.: TGZMBC Tape Library).

3. Rev. Wilfred McKinley served as interim pastor of the Greater Zion Missionary Baptist Church in Harrisburg, Pennsylvania, from 1987 to 1988. He often reminded the congregation of God's sovereignty with this quote.

4. The late Rev. Edward Victor Hill was the guest lecturer at the Evangel Temple Minister's Conference in Baltimore (c. 1988–89) prior to Evangel Temple's relocation to its current location in Upper Marlboro, Maryland.

## Imperative 4: Be Discerning

1. Roland Martin live event special, "What Would Jesus Really Do?" CNN.com transcript, 2007, 1–11.

2. Most of us would welcome a timely unexpected bailout, but there is no lesson to be learned from that kind of largess. There is something to be said for acquiring a discipline in our finances that will hopefully translate into other areas of our lives. Alternatively, several hundred churches nationwide offer members resources through the church's membership in the National Federation of Community Development Credit Unions (NFCDCU; www.natfed.org). This organization (which has a special faith-based program) provides resources primarily for first-time home ownership, small business development, college education, or job training. Through these and other strategies, not only does the church leadership practice discernment in addressing a real need in the congregation, but the members also learn discernment in their future financial choices.

3. Bill Gates, "Unleashing the Power of Creativity," National Public Radio, September 19, 2005, http://www.npr.org/templates/story/story.php?storyId=4853839.

4. Jessica Yadegaran, "Savvy, Stylish, and Plus Size," http://www.campuscircle.com/review.cfm?r=2632, 2006 (accessed November 13, 2007).

5. Mackenzie Carpenter, "For many women, finding plus-size clothes is still a reach," http://www.post-gazette.com/pg/06143/692258-28.stm, May 23, 3006 (accessed November 13, 2007).

## Imperative 5: Be Complementary

1. David L. Laubach, *12 Steps to Congregational Transformation: A Practical Guide for Leaders* (Valley Forge, PA: Judson Press, 2006), 76–77.

2. Ibid., 81.

3. Carol J. Loomis, "A Conversation with Warren Buffet," CNN Money.com, June 25, 2006.

4. James H. Cone, *Martin and Malcolm and America: A Dream or Nightmare?* (Maryknoll, NY: Orbis, 1993), 264.

5. Spencer Johnson, *Who Moved My Cheese?* (New York: G. P. Putnam's Sons, 1998).

6. "Our History," Oak Cliff Bible Fellowship, https://www.ocbfchurch.org/images/uploads/history/19881993.png (accessed October 28, 2007).

## Imperative 6: Be Uncompromising

1. Ted Baehr, Susan Wales, and Ken Wales, *The Amazing Grace of Freedom* (Green Forest, AR: New Leaf Press, 2007), 56–59.

2. David Kay Johnston, "Dozens of the Wealthy Join to Fight Estate Tax Repeal," *New York Times,* February 14, 2001, cited in CommonDreams.org News Center, http://www.commmondreams.org/headlines01/0214-01.htm.

## Imperative 7: Be Encouraged

1. William Whiston, trans., *The Works of Josephus* (Peabody, MA: Hendrickson, 1987), 18.5.116–19; p. 484.

2. "Antoinette Louisa Brown," http://en.wikipedia.org/wiki/Antoinette_Brown (accessed January 22, 2008).

3. President Kennedy's Special Message to the Congress on Urgent National Needs, May 25, 1961.

4. James M. Washington, *A Testament of Hope: The Essential Writings and Speeches of Martin Luther King, Jr.* (New York: Harper-Collins, 1986), 286.

# ABOUT THE AUTHOR

**W**hether you lead in the church or the community, the classroom or the boardroom, there are some essentials you must know. Some might call them principles, but author, speaker, and real-world leader Joseph Robinson Jr. believes they are much more. He has identified what he calls seven leadership *imperatives*, gleaned from the life of the biblical figure, John the Baptist.

Joe Robinson is passionate about helping people identify and cultivate these vital characteristics of leadership. His 26 years of experience in the "real world," working as a division manager for the Commonwealth of Pennsylvania, provided him with a laboratory for implementing these imperatives. For more than two decades with the Pennsylvania Department of Transportation, Joe honed his supervisory, mentoring, and communication skills, and was certified as a quality manager through the American Society for Quality. He understands business and the challenges inherent with delivering quality products and services.

As a deacon at his church, The Greater Zion Missionary Baptist Church in Harrisburg, Pennsylvania, Joe also appreciates how leadership characteristics in the real world translate into the church and ministry setting. He knows from experience that effective leadership at all levels is essential.

In 2006, Joe took an early retirement to focus on a speaking and writing ministry to help equip others with the knowledge and tools they need to lead in their own world. To learn more about Joe's workshops and seminars on leadership topics including the 7 leadership imperatives, strategic planning, team building, and conflict resolution, please visit his website at www.josephrobinsonjr.com. To inquire about speaking engagements, consulting services, or scheduling a workshop or seminar in your area, contact Joe personally!

E-mail:   Jrobin2009@aol.com
Mail:     2009 Bradley Drive
          Harrisburg, PA 17110
Home:    (717) 652-8946
Cell:     (717) 919-4392